THE GRAN PARADISO
AND SOUTHERN VALDOTAIN
The long distance walks

Plan de la Feya on the Entrelor path
with the Colle di Finestra visible across the valley

THE GRAN PARADISO
AND SOUTHERN VALDOTAIN

The long distance walks

by
J.W. Akitt

CICERONE PRESS
MILNTHORPE, CUMBRIA

© J.W. Akitt 1997
ISBN 1 85284 247 4
A catalogue record for this book is available from the British Library.

DEDICATION

To my wife Jean,
who can now undertake and enjoy
only the easier of the walks described here.

ACKNOWLEDGEMENTS

I wish to acknowledge the help given me by several people: G.G. Watkins, librarian of the Fell and Rock Climbing Club who directed me towards some relevant literature; The Alpine Club, who allowed me to consult their library; Signor Enrico Mauro of Aosta who explained the mysteries of the Via Alta 4 to me; and the many anonymous assistants in Italian tourist offices who provided me with all sorts of information which has helped to make this guide as accurate as it can be with respect to telephone numbers and the addresses of accommodation and campsites. Finally, I thank my wife for reading the typescript.

Séez, 1997

Front Cover: Lac d'Arpy and Grandes Jorasses

CONTENTS

Advice to Readers

Readers are advised that whilst every effort is taken by the author to ensure the accuracy of this guidebook, changes can occur which may affect the contents. It is advisable to check locally on transport, accommodation, shops etc but even rights-of-way can be altered.

The publisher would welcome notes of any such changes

PREFACE

The Gran Paradiso was explored in the now distant past by British mountaineers and has since been visited principally by people wishing to climb the peaks. Some walking was done but it is not until recently that English language walking guides have started to appear - three within the last four years. This is surprising since several long distance walks are well established in the Gran Paradiso and adjacent areas and continental walkers are well aware of the region's possibilities. One meets few British people here and it is to be hoped that this, and the other guides, will entice many more to venture into this magnificent mountain region.

The author lives in France but only an hour's drive from La Thuile so that to visit the region is a simple undertaking. His explorations of the Tarentaise Alps brought him first into touch with some of the walks on the Italian side of the frontier and this whetted his appetite for more. In fact, only about half of the mountains across the border from the Tarentaise are in the Gran Paradiso National Park but there is excellent walking outside the park, as well as within. The author quickly became aware of the two Via Alta and then the Grand Traverse and decided that here was a challenge to complete these long walks and so explore this beautiful region. It is hoped that others will share this challenge.

The walking in the Gran Paradiso and southern Valdotain is quite demanding but is within the reach of all fit and reasonably experienced walkers - after all, the author is a pensioner! The only exceptions to this statement are found on two stages of the Via Alta 4 which each have two sections of unusual difficulty. One is protected by a fixed chain but the other three are not, and each places the walker in a situation of exposure with relatively poor footing. These places are discussed in the text and the reader should consider carefully whether his ability permits him to cross them. One should nevertheless not be put off attempting the Via Alta 4 as it is a splendid route, and all the the difficult points can be avoided by taking sections of the easier Via Alta 2.

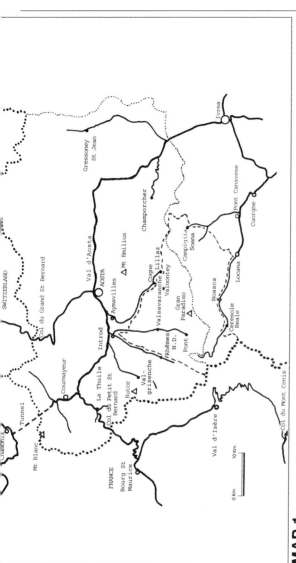

MAP 1.

The layout of the principal roads in the Val d'Aosta, the Valdotain and the Gran Paradiso National Park. The extent of the latter is shown by a dashed line. The Heavy dotted line is the international border between Italy and France or Switzerland. The lightly dotted line is the internal boundary between the Valdotain and the other neighbouring provinces of Italy. Milan is 100km east of Ivrea and Turin is about 45km south.

The Tormotta lake, looking from the path towards Mt Ouille.
The Tormotta itself is to the right, off the picture (see p129)

INTRODUCTION

This book has been written to introduce English speaking fellwalkers to the the major continuous tours and walks which cross this magnificent mountainous region of north-west Italy. It is a complex region which lies next to the Massif of Mt Blanc and indeed contains two of the Alps' 4000m peaks, the highest of which, the Gran Paradiso, gives its name to the national park. In the west it touches the French Tarentaise region over a large distance along the frontier, making this guide a continuation in effect of my earlier Tarentaise guide (J.W. Akitt, *Walking in the Tarentaise & Beaufortain Alps* [Cicerone 1995]). The area is well known to continental walkers and many Italian, French and Dutch people will be encountered, though few British. There is extensive documentation in Italian, some in French and only a little recent work in English.

The area to be described lies south of the Aosta valley and the principal town, Aosta. Map 1 shows how the region is situated relative to France and Switzerland whose borders with Italy form the western and northern limits respectively. These are two continuous mountain barriers along which are found many famous peaks, Mt Blanc and the Matterhorn among many others. Road access to Switzerland is via the Col du Grand St Bernard and access to France is via the Mt Blanc Tunnel or via the Col du Petit St Bernard which latter takes you over into the Tarentaise Alps. To the east, motorways take you via Ivrea towards the cities of Milan or Turin, the nearest large population centres.

The major part of the region to be described lies in the province of Aosta, which has a special statute as the Automonous Region of the Valle d'Aosta. Curiously, this province is roughly rectangular in shape but is held, with a little imagination, to resemble a St Bernard dog in outline, though the legs are short. One could be forgiven for envisaging a Scotch terrier, but as the St Bernard has such a hold on legend in its region of origin, it is pleasant to stretch the imagination, and the legs, a little further. To take the imagery even further, we also see that this St Bernard seems about to chase the hen of Savoie, a feature explained in my Tarentaise guide. The region enclosed by the watershed of the Aosta valley is known as the Valdotain (Ital.

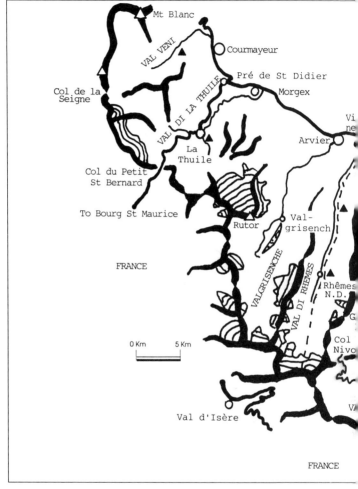

MAP 2.

The southern Valdotain and the northern part of the Province of Turin covered by this guide, showing the principal roads and the main mountain ridges and valleys. The dashed line shows the

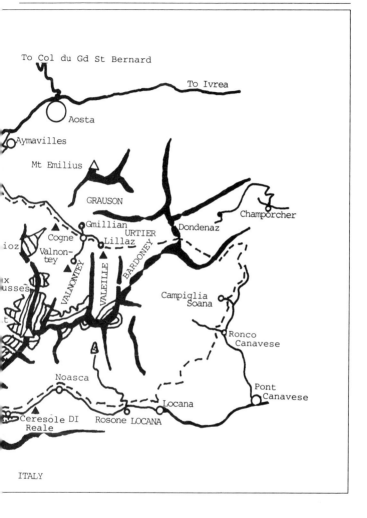

borders of the National Park. Places with accommodation in albergi which are mentioned in the text are indicated, as well as localities with campsites ▲ . Names of valleys are in capitals.

13

Valdostana) and we shall be exploring in this guide the southern Valdotain and as far as the Locana valley, which is in the province of Turin. About half the area is taken up in the east by the Gran Paradiso National Park.

In Map 2 we zoom in onto the area to be covered and can see in more detail the layout of the valley and ridge system. A continuous ridge, with many points in excess of 3000m in altitude, runs south from the Massif of Mt Blanc then turns a little east to near Val d'Isère. This ridge marks the Franco-Italian frontier which turns south here. A big spur however runs east into Italy to form the south wall of the Locana valley. Several high ridges run generally north and east from the frontier ridge to form Val Veni, Valle di la Thuile, Valgrisenche, Val di Rhêmes and Valsavaranche. A much bigger ridge and spur system runs from the Col del Nivolet to near Champorcher and defines the upper Vallon di Cogne and its extensions, the Urtier and Valnontey, as well as the north wall of the Locana valley and many smaller valleys. The culminating point of this ridge system is the Gran Paradiso itself. Below is a short commentary describing each of the principal valleys in turn. It should be noted in passing that the rivers do not always have the same name as the valleys in which they run, viz. the Dora Baltea flows in the Aosta valley, Torrente Grand Eyvia in the Vallon di Cogne and the Torrente Orco in the Locana valley. Though in the case of the last signposts are seen to "Valle d'Orco" (Locana valley) in Pont Canavese and I will use the names interchangeably.

Val Veni runs below the south wall of the massif of Mt Blanc and is a magnificent walk. The Tour of Mt Blanc long distance walk follows part of the valley. The Col de la Seigne connects with France and the Colle di Chavannes with the La Thuile valley to the south.

Valle di la Thuile is an open valley which branches off the Val d'Aosta at Pré de St Didier. A road takes you from here via La Thuile to the Col du Petit St Bernard and France. To the north, Mt Blanc is hidden by the mountains of Mt Bério Blanc and its companions. To the south rises the impressive bulk of the Testa del Rutor (3486m) and its big glacier which forms an obstacle to be turned on the way to Valgrisenche. La Thuile itself is a busy town, besieged by tourists in summer and skiers in winter so that it boasts plenty of accommodation. There are some very pleasant spots around La

14

Thuile and magnificent waterfalls below the Rutor glacier.

The following valleys are all narrow gorges with rocky sides, magnificent or severe according to taste. They all reach deep into the mountains.

Valgrisenche is reached by a road from Arvier which goes to Valgrisenche village then climbs to Bonne above the reservoir of Beauregard. It continues to Surier at the head of the lake using a new road to the west. There is an old road on the east side of the lake but this is narrow and awkward in places. There are cols which lead to the French Tarentaise, the Col du Mont and the Col du Vaudet (which has several names) principally. There is magnificent scenery at the head of the valley and a refuge, the Bezzi, with a gastronomic reputation.

Val di Rhêmes is reached by road from Villeneuve. There are two principal villages, Rhêmes St George and Rhêmes Notre Dame. Again, there is a magnificent glacier cirque at the valley head. The limit of the national park follows the trough of the valley.

Valsavaranche is also served by road from Villeneuve through the village of Dégioz as far as the hamlet of Pont where the altitude attains almost 2000m.

The head of the valley is surrounded by glaciated mountains, the Gran Paradiso itself, the Ciaforon and the sharp Cima de Breuil among others. Less evidently, an elevated, hanging valley, the Piano del Nivolet, runs south-west from Pont to the col del Nivolet, a region where there are many attractive lakes of all sizes. The col is traversed by a road which climbs up from Ceresole Reale but which stops a little after the summit - there is no connection with the road that climbs from Pont in this direction.

Vallon di Cogne is reached by road from Aymavilles which leads to the principal town Cogne with satellites Lillaz, Gmillian and Valnontey. There is thus plenty of accommodation here also. The valley continues past Lillaz as the Vallone di Urtier, which has several attractive side valleys, some of which are shown. The village of Valnontey is some 3km to the south of Cogne, in the valley of the same name, and is distinguished by the presence of the alpine garden "Paradisia". This is well worth a visit, particularly early in the season when it is very pretty. The name derives from a flower common in the region, a small white lily called St Bruno's Lily or, botanically, *Paradisia liliastrum*. The Torrente Valnontey is crossed by a bridge here and there is parking above and below the bridge. It is possible to drive only a little further up the valley.

The head of the valley is made up of a cirque of magnificent glaciated mountains, the Gran Paradiso itself and the Testa di Valnontey, among others.

Valle di Locana is reached by road from Pont Canavese. It runs roughly east-west and the road continues right to the head of the valley, crosses the Col del Nivolet and descends a little to the Lagi del Nivolet. This valley is an enormous contrast to the gorges just described. The Locana valley is wide and pastoral, even in its upper reaches, with villages here and there. The reservoir at Ceresole Reale is very pleasant and the village of Ceresole Reale itself (Royal Ceresole, because of its connections with the hunter king Victor Emanuel II) is spread out, with plenty of accommodation. Lower down the valley there is a monument to chimney sweeps by the roadside. It was traditional in Savoie (and here we are in what was a part of Savoie prior to 1860) to send the older boys of a family to sweep chimneys in winter. This meant less mouths to feed in the hard times and possibly a little money extra in the spring.

A road runs north from the village of Rosone as far as the dam of the Lago di Telecchio and gives easy access to the Rif. Pontese and to the ridges around.

Valle di Soana is also reached by road from Pont Canavese. This is a wooded valley with several towns, and accommodation at Campiglia Soana where the road ends, which is also a starting or finishing point for the original version of the long distance walk called the Grand Traverse of the Gran Paradiso.

Valle di Champorcher is a short valley which is entered by the road that starts near Donnas, north of Ivrea. It runs in a westerly direction to a group of hamlets known collectively as Champorcher, the last two you encounter being the hamlets of Chateau and Chardonnay. There is a fork right at Chateau which takes you up the valleyside then traverses as far as Dondenaz, in sight of the refuge of the same name.

All these valleys are connected by two or more cols which cross the intervening ridges and the long distance walks cross these from valley to valley.

ACCESS AND ACCOMMODATION

Access by air is possible to either Milan or Turin. There are trains to Aosta or direct to Pont Canavese from Turin or with a change at Ivrea if travelling from Milan. There are buses, in season, from Aosta to all the northern valleys and from Pont Canavese to Ceresole Reale or as far as the Col del Nivolet on Sundays and to Ronco Canavese.

The train journey has of course been revolutionised by the Channel Tunnel. Go London - Paris - Bourg St Maurice, a journey which can be done within the day. There are buses from Bourg to Aosta or La Thuile, or it is possible to walk into Italy from France over one of the many cols.

By car, the most direct approach is via Chamonix and the Mt Blanc Tunnel (the toll can be paid in either French francs or Italian lire) into the Val d'Aosta. Once you are established in one of the valleys you will probably find that the car is of limited use since much of the walking is done valley to valley, though a vehicle could be very useful out of season.

Accommodation within the valleys themselves is adequate and is in albergi (cheap hotels) or on campsites. The albergi need not be expensive and some are little dearer than dinner, bed and breakfast at a refuge. A refuge currently costs typically 55,000 lire per person and an albergo from about 60,000 lire. Details can be had from the tourist offices listed below. A non-exhaustive list of albergi is also given and a list of campsites. Note that camping is forbidden in the national park outside the designated campsites. Refuges will be discussed a little later.

List of tourist offices

LA THUILE - Via Collombe, 11016 Aosta. Tel: 0165 884 179

VILLENEUVE - To north of main road in Val d'Aosta. 11018 Aosta. Tel: 0165 959 75

RHEMES NOTRE DAME - Centre visites Parc National Grand Paradis. Open only in summer. Tel: 0165 905 808.

GOGNE - Piazza Chanoux, 11012 Aosta. Tel: 0165 740 40

CERESOLE REALE - On the main road, near the town hall.
Tel: 0124 95186/95121
COURMAYEUR - Piazzale Monte Bianco, 11013 Aosta.
Tel: 0165 842 060
AOSTA - Piazza Chanoux, 11100 Aosta. Tel: 0165 40526/35655

Some cheaper hotels or albergi

The regional code is 0165 for all but those in the Locana valley, where it is 0124.

LA THUILE - There are 10 one and two star hotels to choose from: Chalet Alpina (Tel: 884187), Edelweiss (Tel: 884144), Entrèves (Tel: 884134), Genzianella (Tel: 884137), Martinet (Tel: 884656), Miravidi (Tel: 884112), Piccolo S. Bernardo (Tel: 884539), Rolland (Tel: 884565), Soggiorno Firenze (Tel: 884338) and Belvedere (Tel: 884155).

VALGRISENCHE - Several hotels spread about the valley between Planaval and Bonne: Paramont at Planaval (Tel: 97106), Maison des Myrtilles at Chez Carral (Tel: 97118), Gran Sassière at Gerbelle (Tel: 97113), Frassy in Valgrisenche village (Tel: 97100) and Perret at Bonne (Tel: 97107).

VAL DI RHEMES - Several hotels in and around Rhêmes Notre Dame: Galisa, in the village (Tel: 936100), Grand Rousse (Tel: 936105), Della Pineta (Tel: 936101), Pellaud, at the hamlet of the same name (Tel: 936110). There are also bed and breakfast places in the village.

VALSAVARANCHE - There are three hotels at Pont: Fior di Roccia (Tel: 95478) is one star, Genzianella (Tel: 95393) and Gran Paradiso (Tel: 95454) are three star. L'Hostellerie du Paradis is at Eaux Rousses (Tel: 905972).

VALLON DI COGNE - Very many hotels at Cogne itself and at nearby Gmillian, Lillaz and Valnontey, with 18 in the cheaper categories. Evidently it would be wise to enlist the help of the tourist office to find a place. I give a few names below for those who wish to book by telephone: at Cogne, Au Vieux Grenier (Tel: 74002); at Gmillian, Grauson (Tel: 74001), Belvedere (Tel: 74059); at Valnontey, Paradisia (Tel: 74158), Valereusa (Tel: 749202); at Lillaz, Ondezana (Tel: 74248).

VALLE DI LOCANA - At Ceresole Reale there are 10 albergi with the cheapest being Ciaforon (Tel: 953122), Gran Paradiso (Tel: 953221), Pineta (Tel: 953110) and Sport (Tel: 953187). Note that all these hotels are at altitudes of between 1350 and 2000m and are all well into the mountains.

List of campsites
Telephone code 0165

LA THUILE - Camping Rutor, Tel: 884165. In the direction of La Joux.

VAL DI RHÊMES - Camping Marmotta, Tel: 936118. Situated at Rhêmes Notre Dame, on the left when entering the village if going up the valley.
Camping Val di Rhêmes, Tel: 907648. At Rhêmes St Georges.

VALSAVARANCHE - Camping Grivola, Tel: 905743. Situated down the valley from Eaux Rousses.
Camping Gran Paradiso, Tel: 95433. Situated about half way between Eaux Rousses and Pont, on the eastern side of the valley where a road bridge crosses the river. Called Plan de la Pesse on map.
Camping Pont-Breuil, Tel: 95458. Situated at Pont at the end of the road up Valsavaranche. A particularly large site.

VALLON DI COGNE - There are several sites in the valleys around Cogne and one at Cogne itself.
At Cogne: Vallée de Cogne, Tel: 74079. Situated at the entrance to the village.
At Valnontey: Camping Bouva, Tel: 74181.
Camping lo Stambecco, Tel: 74152.
Camping Gran Paradiso, Tel: 749 204.
At Lillaz: Camping al Sole, Tel: 74237.
Camping les Salasses, Tel: 74252.
There is also a site at Epinel but this was temporarily closed at time of writing.

CERESOLE REALE - Telephone code 0124. There are three sites strung out along the valley:
Camping Piccolo Paradiso, Tel: 953 235, Camping Villa, Tel: 953 212 and Camping la Peschera, Tel: 953 222.
There are also many sites in the Aosta valley at Courmayeur, Morgex, La Salle, Avise, Arvier, Villeveuve, Sarre etc.

WHEN TO GO

The alpine walking season traditionally is said to extend from mid June to mid September. The reasoning behind this is that before and after these dates, the previous winter's snow may remain frozen all day, especially at the higher altitudes, and so be dangerous to cross without the aid of appropriate equipment such as ice axe and/or crampons. This view does not, however, take account of an asymmetry in the seasons; there will be much less snow left on the ground in September than will be encountered in June so that snow is much less likely to be an obstacle in the early autumn. The walks in the Gran Paradiso mostly go rather high - there are many cols in excess of 3000m in altitude - and these are likely to be under snow in May or June. Indeed, the Italian guidebooks often suggest that these high walks should not be attempted before mid July. As a result, the region is at its busiest in August when advanced booking of accomodation is essential. July and August are also the hottest months. Many British walkers will thus find the autumn the most pleasant time to walk here though there is always the risk of bad weather with new snow at high altitude, and most refuges are closed by the end of September. Walks of a single day's duration will nevertheless be very rewarding in the autumn.

Another consideration, important for some British walkers at least, is the beauty of the alpine flower display. This is best in July and August and, with a few late exceptions, the flowers are fading fast by early September so autumnal holidaymakers will miss them. The Alps are also very green in high summer but by mid September the vegetation starts to die back in anticipation of the rigours of winter, and the slopes turn brown to take on an appearance more akin to that of the British hills. Choose mid July through to October depending upon your priorities and the flexibility of your holidays.

THE WEATHER

The weather in all mountain areas is less reliable than on the surrounding plains, and the Alps are no exception to this rule though the weather is generally better than on British hills and particularly in the July-August holiday period. Generalising, one can say that May and June in the Alps are mixed, though June can be very pleasant. July and August are sunny and hot with short periods of rainy weather, while September and October are cooler but often fine. The weather in July and August is, however, different in many ways from that of a good British summer. It tends to fall into one of two patterns which may succeed one another. Long periods of up to perhaps ten days of brilliant, often cloudless skies followed by about three days of rainy weather is one sequence which may be experienced, though the periods of fine weather will be shorter in a poor summer. The sunny days will be hot in the valleys but, since the temperature falls significantly with increasing altitude, it will feel much pleasanter above 2000m. An alternative weather pattern is one of a long series of similar days on which the mornings are brilliantly clear but cloud builds up during the course of the day until some time after 4pm when thunderstorms break out on and around the summits. The clouds disappear overnight. The storms can be very violent and it is as well not be be caught in one, certainly not on a ridge. Such days are nevertheless good for walking, provided the day is arranged so that return to the valley or refuge is made before the storms break out.

It is inadvisable to venture high during really bad weather as it can be very cold at altitude. It is also unnecessary, in view of the likelihood of a quick return of good weather.

One corner of the region which does not appear to obey strictly these rules is the Locana valley. This seems to come more under the influence of the Piedmont plain and can be dull and cloudy when the area to the north-west and the French Tarentaise are having good weather. I have also noted that the older English texts describing expeditions in the Gran Paradiso often talk of rainy conditions and this may be an expression of the same tendency.

Winds are rarely a nuisance in that the sort of gale which requires the walker to lean into it is unusual in summer.

Weather forecasts in the Gran Paradiso are a problem. The refuge guardians to whom I have spoken about this are unanimous that the Italian forecasts are not accurate in the mountains and they telephone Geneva. The forecast from Chamonix should be even better but there is only one number accessible from outside France at the moment. This replied in English in 1995, in French in 1996, and English again in summer 1997. If enough people use it, it will continue in English. The various numbers are:

Phoning from Italy:
    Geneva - 00 41 28 162, in French.
    Chamonix - 00 33 478 580 042, in English one hopes!

Phoning from France:
    Chamonix - 04 78 58 00 42, in English.

In addition, there are forecasts available in France for each department. These have the numbers 08 36 68 02 xx, where xx is the number of the department for which you need the forecast. Thus xx=74 gets you Haute Savoie, ie. Chamonix, while xx=73 gets you Savoie, ie. Bourg St Maurice. These numbers are not available outside France at the time of writing but are expected to be so sometime in 1998. This could be useful in that the forecast for Savoie is possibly better for the southern part of the region. Unfortunately, the number gives you various alternatives to try and you need to be quite fluent in French to use it effectively.

The Foehn effect
If the wind blows from the south, up the boot of Italy, this often establishes a foehn wind in the mountains. Such a wind will be warm and carry much moisture from the Mediterranean. When it reaches the Alps it is forced to rise and so is cooled and starts to lose its moisture content as rain or snow, depending on the season. The precipitation on the Italian slopes of the Alps can be very heavy under these conditions. The wind escapes through the cols and descends on the other side as a warm dry wind which can be very strong. The foehn thus produces generally disagreeable conditions with a sharp change in the type of perturbation as one crosses the frontier ridge. Fortunately, the foehn is not common in summer but is an autumn to spring phenomenon.

MAPS AND BOOKS
The best maps to use for walking seem to me to be the IGC (Istituto Geographico Centrale) 1:25,000 series. Three are required to cover the region: No.101 (Gran Paradiso, Grivola, Cogne), No.102 (Valsavaranche, Val di Rhêmes, Valgrisenche) and No.107 (Monte Bianco, Courmayeur, Chamonix, La Thuile). These show much of

the detail of the terrain though the vertical interval of the contours is quite coarse at 25m. Some paths are marked in black - usually with accuracy - and others are in red using lines of various thicknesses. Thin dashed lines seem to indicate paths which are not too well demarked. Three long distance walks are marked by a thick red line, these being the Via Alta 2, Via Alta 4 and the Grande Traversée des Alpes which will not concern us here. As far as the two Via Alta are concerned, it is important to realise that these thick lines do not mean that the paths they designate are everywhere excellent and easy - they have easy and difficult sections - but that they are at the top of a heirarchy of paths. In addition, the lines are not drawn very accurately and often show simply the general direction to be taken. The waymarking system helps to make up for this inaccuracy. IGC also publishes a map at 1:50,000, No.3, Il Parco Nazionale Del Gran Paradiso. This covers the whole of the area in one map, including the Bellacomba lakes south of La Thuile which are missing from the 1:25,000 series. Unfortunately, the vertical interval is 100m which is not sufficiently accurate for serious routefinding. The path marking is similar to that of the large scale series above and some different paths are shown on the two IGC series. Another 1:50,000 map is published by Studio F.M.B. Bologna, entitled Gran Paradiso. It is similar to the ICG map through many more footpaths are marked - with little improvement in accuracy - and the reverse is printed with much useful information in Italian, though some telephone numbers are now out of date. The names are also more Italianised on this map than on the IGC series. This is the only map which shows the Grand Traversata del Gran Paradiso as a long distance walk.

The inaccuracies of the IGC 1:25,000 maps is annoying and I have attempted to make up for this in my sketch maps. However, it has quite recently come to my attention that maps which have been bought later than mine have had corrections and changes made. When I note discrepancies in these maps this applies to the three in my possession, not necessarily those that you, the reader, may buy!

Some French maps are also useful for the western edge of the region. Didier & Richard No.8, Massifs du Mt Blanc-Beaufortain, at 1:50,000 covers the La Thuile valley very well with a contour interval in Italy of 25m. No.11 in the same series, Vanoise, covers the tour of the Archeboc. The IGN TOP25 No.3531ET, St Gervais, at 1:25,000 covers the northern part of the La Thuile valley with a contour interval of 20m in Italy. No.3532ET, Les Arcs, La Plagne, in the same series covers the French side of the tour of the Archeboc and also the route between the Col du Tachuy and the Col du Mont. The only other maps which depict these routes are the D&R series.

These maps can all be bought locally in either France of Italy, though many prefer to plan ahead and purchase maps before they leave for the Alps. Your local hillsports shop should be able to order them for you, or they can be obtained from Stanfords Ltd, 12 Long Acre, London WC2, The Map Shop, Upton-on-Severn, World Leisure Marketing & Mapworld, Westmeadows Estate, Derby DE21 6HA .

As for books about the region of interest, there is an extensive literature in Italian, as a visit to any local bookshop will show. I have seen two French books and two recent books in English which have some overlap with this guide. There is quite an extensive older English literature going back into the 19th century, and two which were published after the last war are of general interest to the visitor though they deal more with mountaineering than with walking.

A selection of Italian texts:

L. Fachin, *Il Parco Nazionale Del Gran Paradiso,* Musumechi Editore, Aosta (1992)

G. Berutto, *Il Parco Nazionale Del Gran Paradiso,* Istituto Geografico Centrale, Turin (undated). Vol.1, Valli Soana - Orco - Rhêmes - Valgrisenche

P. Giglio and P. Orsieres, *Valle d'Aosta,* CDA

French texts:

G.L. Grassi, *Le Grand Paradis et Lanzo,* Denoel, Paris (1982). A French translation of an Italian book which describes walks in the area and to the south.

B. Brunet, *Randonnées Entre Vanoise et Mont Blanc,* l'Edelweiss, Bourg St Maurice (1993), describes several outings in the Gran Paradiso as well as in France.

English texts:

J.G.R. Harding, *Alpine Journal,* 82, pp 133-143 (1977), gives a history of climbing in the area.

J. Adam Smith, *Mountain Holidays*, Dent & Sons (1946) reissued by
    the Ernest Press (1996)
M.R. Lieberman, *Walking the Alpine Parks of France & Northern Italy*,
    The Mountaineers, Washington (1994)
G. Price, *Walking in Italy's Gran Paradiso*, Cicerone (1997)

LANGUAGE

It is clear that the question of whether to use French or Italian poses
a continual problem, and indeed both languages are still used
currently and officially in the Valdotain. The reasons for this duality
are embedded in history. In 35 BC Julius Caesar decided that he, or
Rome, needed a land route into France over the Col du Petit St
Bernard and by 25 BC the Romans had conquered the Valdotain,
which up to then had been independent of Rome. Aosta was
founded as *Augusta Praetoria* and the col the *Alpis Graia*. The Grand
St Bernard was the *Alpis Poenina*. Aosta contains magnificent vestiges
of Rome. After the collapse of the Roman Empire, the Valdotain was
subject to various invaders of which the major influence was that of
Franco-Burgandy which led to the language of the region evolving
into French, which was certainly the official language in the 14th
century, if not earlier.

Around the year 1000 an individual Count called Humbert of
the White Hands started to impose himself upon the region, to such
long lasting effect that he founded the House of Savoie, the longest
unbroken line of rulers in Europe. The Dukes of Savoie ruled over
a country of fluctuating size and importance, much of their influence
arising as the "doorkeepers of the Alps", many of whose cols they
controlled. Over the centuries, however, the Dukes found that their
possessions on the French side of the Alps were difficult to defend
if the French decided to invade (France was the most populous
country in Europe at the time, when the biggest army meant most
power) and began to concentrate on guarding their possessions on
the Italian side of the Alpine Arc. Thus, when the Emperor Napoleon
III, with the treaty of Turin (1860), essentially created the present
state of Italy, the Duke of Savoie became the first king of the new
nation. The French speaking Valdotain to its consternation became
part of Italy with Italian as the official language. The exclusion of
French was practised with varying degrees of severity over the

decades that followed, the fascist dictatorship of Mussolini being particularly intransigent. The French language remained alive, however, and in 1948 the Valdotain became the Automonous Region of the Val d'Aosta where both French and Italian are official languages.

We must also note in passing that in 1860 the part of Savoie on the French side of the Alps was allowed to decide for itself, in a referendum, whether to become part of France or of Italy and evidently choose the former option.

The result of all these historical events is that today, most of the inhabitants of the Valdotain are bilingual, though some may not be too fluent in their second tongue. A knowledge of either tongue is thus very useful, especially as the number of people who can speak English seems limited, not surprisingly so since this demands trilingualsim.

The duality of language is very clear from the maps. Some names are pure French, some are pure Italian and some are mixed. Most names in fact can be expressed in either tongue, the (presumably older) French or the Italian replacement. The English speaking visitor may well be confused by a modern signpost in the mountains indicating in Italian a place named in French on the map. For instance, the glacier col Col de la Noire above the Refuge Vittorio Sella is called Col Nero on a painted rock at the path junction. This duality may cause some problems for those not familiar with the two languages and for this reason, where names are found in several forms on the various maps, the equivalent forms are given in small glossaries at the start of each walk. The French forms of some of the names have the silent endings 'x' or 'z' which is a Savoyard artefact. It means that a Savoyard French name such as Dondenaz is spelt in Italian as Dondena, the pronunciation being exactly the same. I will leave readers to detect these cases for themselves.

The problem appears not to be new. The mountaineer Cowell in 1860 complained that the names of the peaks in the Gran Paradiso were shrouded in obscurity!

The Locana valley is not in the province of Aosta but in that of Turin and despite being part of Savoie in the past is much more Italian, and the language of its inhabitants is Italian. Some of the people you encounter do indeed speak French but this is less likely than in the valleys to the north.

Refuge guardians fortunately tend to be multilingual.

I give below a short glossary of equivalent English, Italian and French terms which are found frequently on the maps. These are not given in the later glossaries where it will be assumed that the equivalence of such terms as lac, lago; col, colle is understood.

Glossary of equivalent French, Italian and English terms found frequently on the maps

ENGLISH	FRENCH	ITALIAN
col, pass	col, cormet	colle, passo
crossing	passage, passeur	-
window, gap	fenêtre	finestra, bocchetta
northern	nord	settentrionale
central	central(e)	centrale
south	sud	meridionale
upper	dessus, d'en haut	alte, di sopra
middle	-	di mezzo
lower	dessous, d'en bas	basse, di sotto
lowest part		di fondo
hillside	côte	costa
glacier	glacier	ghiacciaio
cross (religous)	croix	croce
hunting lodge (royal)	-	casa di caccia (reale)
summit	mt, aiguille, dent tour, pointe, tête...	monte, montagna, punta,becca, testa, torre, guglia...
refuge	refuge (ref.)	rifugio (rif.)
alp		alpi,mgne (montagne)
lake, tarn	lac	lago
waterfall	cascade	cascata

valley	vallée, vallon	vallone
a level place	plan	pian(o)
of	de	di
of the	du, de la	delle, della, dei, etc.
red	rouge, rousse	rosso
mountain stream	torrent, ruisseau, rau	torrente, rio, dora

FOOTPATHS AND WAYMARKING

The network of footpaths which exists today owes much to King Victor Emmanuel II who was a passionate hunter of the ibex and caused many kilometres of mule track to be made to allow the hunters easy access to the higher mountain areas. Eventually, in 1922, these hunting grounds were made a national park in order to protect the fauna. To be clear about the nature of the paths, I use the term "path" to denote a narrow path not wide enough to admit more than two people albreast; a "mule track" is manmade and should be wider but may have become a path; "track" means an unsurfaced road wide enough to take four wheeled vehicles; and "road" means a surfaced road. Note that it is not generally possible to drive high into the mountains in Italy as vehicular access is limited by law. The road endings are denoted by the No Way sign, a red circle with a plain white centre. There are ample car parks at such points.

The Italians have developed to a very fine art the protection of difficult sections of a route by fixed wire or chain handrails. These find their apotheosis in the via ferrata of the Dolomites. There is nothing of this scale in the Gran Paradiso but there are several places where such artificial protection is used, and one or two where progress would be nearly impossible were not some protection in place. Mostly, it is sufficient to use the chain as a handrail, though it is wise to check the anchorage points as you go along; the winter's snow can cause considerable damage and can even wrench a chain right away from the rocks. In the most difficult passages it is customary to protect yourself by means of a waist sling and short length of rope with a large karabiner at its end. This is clipped to the chain and slides along as you move but needs to be unclipped and reattached at the other side of each fixing point encountered. This of course means that, momentarily, you are not protected. Increased security is obtained by using two ropes and karabiners so that you are never unattached.

The waymarking in the Valdotain mountains is comprehensive and complex and can also be confusing. One companion described a rock adorned with some six numbers as a bus stop! In principle, all recognised paths are regularly waymarked with yellow discs outlined in black with a number in the centre. Unfortunately, there was an older system whose numbers also are still to be seen and the maps give some of these older numbers rather than the current ones. The Via Alta are marked in a similar way except that the shape of the yellow background is triangular. Both types of mark appear on sections which double up as a day outing and part of a Via Alta. If the path is difficult to follow - and there are a few of these - yellow splashes of paint will also appear on suitable rocks. In common with all waymarking systems, if you lose the path, you lose the waymarks too so that the arrangement is not perfect. Metallic signposts are also placed at strategic points with yellow finger plates which give destination, time needed to get there and path number. On some of these, however, the lettering is fading and they are difficult, or impossible, to read. On the two Via Alta the waymarks are always the same and are shown in the text as $\Delta 2$ and $\Delta 4$. On day outings the waymark numbers vary and are shown as ¬2, ¬3, etc. Where I have seen any variations in waymarking I mention this if useful.

In the province of Turin the waymarking system seems to be quite different. Wooden fingerposts are used and the waymarking is in dull red slashes of paint, with few exceptions. All over the region one encounters also instructions painted on rocks. Finally, the walker must NOT assume that the waymarking is so comprehensive that the map can be dispensed with. That way disaster lies.

Névé

This is the name given to the remains of last winter's snow and this differentiates the Alps perhaps more than anything else from the walking in the UK. It forms an extensive cover early in the season but melts rapidly each day as the season progresses and may be almost completely absent by the end of August. Its state depends upon many factors such as the extent of the snowfall last winter, the warmth of the spring and the heat of the summer. *Névé* is solid and compacted but has not suffered the transformation to ice that occurs in the glaciers. Its surface becomes rippled, rather like a sea washed beach, and the ripples provide good foothold. When the surface is frozen, as it may be early in the morning, even in high summer, *névé* is dangerous since a slip can lead to an unstoppable fall. Under such conditions it is necessary to use an ice axe and/or crampons to cross the snow. As the day warms up, the surface of the *névé* will soften and it is then practicable to cross. Special equipment is not necessary though many walkers are to be observed using ski poles as an aid. Good, rigid boots are, however, essential on snow as the trainer type of footwear is more prone to slipping. Apart from the obvious danger of a slip and slide, the main danger associated with *névé* is the way it can conceal streams and lakes. The thickness and strength of the snow may be sufficient to hold the weight of a walker early in the season but as the snow melts this assurance becomes less and less reliable. It is therefore imperative **not** to cross *névé* following the bottom of a valley or hollow; always keep up above the lowest part of the slope. The map should also be consulted to see if any lakes are marked as existing under the snow to be crossed and these should be avoided. At the same time remember that not all small lakes are marked and that the maps are not infallible. In addition, be careful at the edge of *névé* or around big rocks showing through the snow as this often melts away from the snow-ground interface and will collapse under your feet, resulting in an unpleasant jolt and wet socks.

Note that if *névé* has melted to expose ice at any significant angle then do not try to cross without the correct equipment.

Despite all these warnings, it should be stated that the Gran Paradiso, despite the high altitude of many of its cols, becomes remarkably clear of *névé* during the summer.

GRADING OF WALKS AND TIME REQUIRED

Giving a walk a grade is fraught with difficulties since it is almost impossible to be completely objective. Despite the limitations, I have assigned the walks one of five grades:

Grade 1   A simple walk on good paths with not too much ascent. Within the capabilities of most people.

Grade 2   A longer but still straightforward expedition, with perhaps some steeper sections.

Grade 3   A walk to high altitude which demands a high degree of fitness. The footpaths may not always be well marked.

Grade 4   As (3) but over difficult terrain and/or in exposed positions. Such walks should be avoided by persons who feel unhappy on Striding Edge or Crib Goch.

Grade 4M   As (4) but where there is an element of objective mountaineering danger. This applies particularly to passages where protection is given by fixed chain or wire.

It cannot be emphasised too much that an individual's reaction to the difficulty of a particular walk depends not only upon the actual difficulties encountered but upon the state of fitness, range of experience, state of fatigue and so on of the person concerned. These grades are then simply indicative of what the author regards as the relative difficulties of the walks and does not exonerate the individual from exercising proper judgement on a particular walk, whatever its given grade, as to whether it is safe to continue given the current snow and weather conditions and degree of fatigue of members of the party.

Timing a walk is less contentious since one simply has to apply a suitable formula to the distance/height-gain mixture to obtain a figure which is incontestable, even if the formula might be! Because the formula chosen will not necessarily apply to a given party, I explain in detail how I have arrived at the times given with each stage of the walks so that parties can make adjustments as necessary for their range of ability.

The majority of the stages and one day walks described cover mostly steep terrain so that the factor which has most influence on time is the altitude gained on the ascent and that lost on the descent.

In many cases it is sufficient to work out the altitudes of departure and arrival and ignore the horizontal distance covered. Where the slopes are very gentle, however, an addition is made for the near horizontal distance covered. The formulae are given below with height gain in metres and time in hours:

1) A long distance stage over steep ground, on the ascent:
   Time needed = height gain ÷ 250
   For the descent:
   Time needed = height loss ÷ 500

2) If there are substantial gently sloping sections an additional time will be added of:
   Time needed = horizontal distance in km ÷ 6
   This implies that if the ascent is less than 41m per km then the time is determined by distance.

3) A day long walk where the rucksack should be appreciably lighter than on a tour:
   Time needed = height gain ÷ 300
   Time for descent will be calculated as in (1) and correction for horizontal distance as in (2) above.

These times are no more than indications of how long a walk may take. Some parties will be slower and some faster and performance will in any case improve as the holiday proceeds. The times given in the Italian literature are usually shorter than those calculated here though a few are about the same. I do not know how these times were obtained. It is also very important to remember that NO allowance has been made in the given times for stops to look at the view, eat, etc. Parties should allow appropriate extra time for such stops.

WALKING STRATEGY

Such a subject may seem surperflous to an experienced walker, but the Alps do have peculiarities not met in the UK. This was emphasised for me on reading a comment written by an English party staying at a friend's apartment in the French Tarentaise: "Too hot for serious walking". Well yes, it was a very hot July, in the valley. Above 2000m altitude, on the other hand, the temperature was much more reasonable. This gives the clue to pleasurable walking in the Alps in

The Trélatête from the Vallone di Chavannes (VA2)

The Lago Djouan from below the Entrelor col. The mountains on the other side of Valsavaranche are the Grivola - (centre) and Grand Nomenon - (left). (VA2)

high summer: make an early start, get high before the day heats up and enjoy the cool of the upper slopes. Ideally, for any long walk to be undertaken in July or August one should aim to set out before 7am (Italian summer time, currently two hours ahead of GMT). The major part of the ascent is made in cool conditions and overheating on the descent is unlikely. In addition, you return early enough to avoid the afternoon thunderstorms if such are forecast.

One very important effect of the heat combined with the altitude and predominance of steep ascents is rapid dehydration. It is thus essential to carry water in one form or another, and I suggest a minimum of 1 litre per person. Many carry the $1^{1}/_{2}$ litre plastic bottles of mineral water available in the shops. It is possible to top up the water at springs, though it is advisable to take care in the choice of such sources. Many streams act as the recipients for the foul water from high altitude chalets and the pollution is increased by the herds which graze on the alps. Nor should water from glacier streams be used as this may contain powdered rock in suspension and is said to give digestive problems. Food should also be carried though what and how much will depend upon individual choice. The guarded refuges provide food and drink to day visitors at not unreasonable prices and a meal at such places can make a very welcome pause.

A second essential for the fair skinned Briton is some protection from sunburn. The sun in the clear air of the mountains is very intense and, in any case, contains more UV light than at sea level. A good sunburn cream should thus be applied to all exposed skin and renewed as necessary. I find the waterproof creams to be best since they resist being washed off by perspiration. Sunglasses are optional unless you expect to spend much time on or near snow when they are essential as the reflected light can be very intense.

It should go without saying that any visitor to the Alps should be fit upon arrival, the best way of ensuring this being to undertake some walks before leaving the UK. Even then it is wise to take account of the effects of heat and altitude on performance and work yourself in, early in the tour. The clothing needed is similar to that which is suitable for walking in the UK. Certainly, take something warm and windproof in case the party are surprised by bad weather. This is emphasised since the drop in temperature which occurs with an adverse change in the weather is much more marked than is usual in the UK. At the same time expect it to be hot, particularly on the ascent, and wear light clothing with the rest in reserve in the rucksack. Shorts are ideal in high summer and some even use bathing suits, but warm clothing must be carried. As far as footwear is concerned, the easier walks should provide no difficulties to people wearing trainer type shoes but I would strongly advise that for the higher grade walks some form of boot be worn with Vibram type sole, capable of coping with rough or wet ground and giving some support for the ankle.

One question to be settled by any party is whether to set out in poor weather. If this occurs during a tour there may not be much choice, unless the weather is so bad that one is inevitably stuck in the refuge. In the case of a day outing, however, it is probably best not to go out if the day is poor. By that I mean rain or imminent rain. The weather is generally so good that it is not really necessary to take the risk involved, since there is a good chance of an improvement soon. It is also a shame to miss the scenic value of the Alps. Remember that the adage 'rain before seven, fine before eleven' has no relevance here as it is unusual for a poor morning to clear quickly. On the other hand, a bad weather patch can clear progressively during a day. Nor should one be put off by valley cloud which leaves the tops clear.

It is also worth mentioning the perennial problem of foot care. Most people will take with them the materials that they know to be effective for them, but if it is necessary to buy locally in Italy there are one or two points that it might be useful to know. Firstly, Elastoplast is not known as such in Italy though a range of similar dressings are sold under proprietary names. It is best to show the pharmacist an example of what is required. On the other hand it is possible to buy Elastoplast-E, which is a linen type bandage with one adhesive face and is used to protect known vulnerable points, prior to any damage occurring. Compeed patches for treatment of blisters are also available in Italy.

There is a significant adder population in these Alps though one seldom sees them. Anti-venom serum is available though it seems to be agreed that in the field this can be more dangerous than the bite itself. The best precaution is to carry a suction kit called Succhiaveleno. If bitten, suck out as much venom as possible using the kit, then walk back to the valley for assistance, without hurrying and with a light tourniquet applied to the bitten limb.

SECURITY

Many of the causes of accidents to walkers will already be familiar to the reader: fatigue, getting benighted or losing the way can all lead to the need for assistance. Falling on *névé* is not usually a problem in the UK but can be particularly grave in its consequences if the victim encounters rocks on the way down. The possibility of falling through snow bridges has already been discussed; the risk is minimised by avoiding snow filled hollows and the bottoms of snow filled valleys or gulleys. One significant risk in the Alps is that of slipping and falling on steep, grassy slopes which have become wet due to rainfall. Avoid the temptation to cross such slopes in the absence of a path as foothold can be meagre and there is real danger of rolling a long way. Care should be exercised on scree which is encountered commonly in the Gran Paradiso. It is best not to try and run it on the descent and a lookout should be kept at all times for falling stones which can be a danger both to yourselves and others. In particular, keep close together on scree.

On a descent, do not go down a convex slope where the lower part is not visible to you - a steep cliff may be hidden from you. This is a particularly important rule to follow in the Gran Paradiso as many of the paths traverse steep, rocky ground and make their way along the easier passages through small cliffs. It is not advisable to take short cuts in this type of terrain.

Mountain rescue is reached by phoning: Valdotain - (0165) 34 983; Locana valley - (0124) 953 188.

Streams emerging from glaciers can also present problems. The flow will normally be reduced early in the morning due to the night's frost, and it may be quite easy to cross at an unbridged point. Later in the day, however, the sun will have caused the ice to melt and the flow will be much augmented so that it may be impossible to cross if the return is to be made that way. The route should be chosen to use what bridges are available. Indeed, many of the glaciers in this region feed such large rivers that crossing is only possible at bridges.

In three of the valleys, the Locana, Champorcher and

Valgrisenche, there are hydroelectric works and the streams are used to convey water as needed by the system. The water can thus rise extremely rapidly in such streams if a sluice is opened somewhere. The danger points are indicated by signs consisting of a red triangle surmounting a square notice which warns of the danger in several languages, including English.

It could be useful to have at least one ice axe with a party, provided someone knows how to use it! The use of ski poles has become very fashionable and can give extra push uphill and protect knees on the way down. It is also possible to use a ski pole to arrest a slip on *névé*. Grasp the pole near the basket with one hand and place the other as high up the pole as possible. Jam the point in the snow and weigh on it, keeping the pole vertical to the snow. Do not forget to try and obtain purchase with the feet at the same time.

REFUGES AND BIVOUACS

There are many mountain refuges within the area. Almost all are guarded and provide simple bunkhouse accommodation with dinner and breakfast. They are very busy in the height of the season and it is essential to book in advance if you want a place. Details and telephone numbers are given below and the location is shown on Map 3. Refuges may be privately operated or belong to the Club Alpino Italiano. They are open from mid June to mid or end September and you should check this if walking late in the season. Some have unguarded winter accommodation.

Bivacci (bivouacs) are small, unguarded shelters and are usually of metallic construction. Many are situated strategically at the start of mountaineering routes and are not therefore of much use to the readers of this book though to walk up to a bivacco can make a good day with a close approach to the mountains and glaciers. Preferably, return the same day as to stay overnight may inconvenience others who wish to go higher. If using a bivouac, it is necessary to take food though blankets are provided. A torch and sheet sleeping bag should be taken to refuge or bivouac.

These shelters are marked on the Italian maps as

Rif. = rifugio or refuge
Biv. = bivacco or bivouac (do not confuse with bivio = junction)
Ric. = ricovero or shelter
Rov. = rovina or ruined. Do not try and stay here!

List of refuges

La Thuile

1) Elizabetta Soldini. Alt. 2200m, 85 beds. Tel: (0165) 844080. C.A.I. Situated on the Tour de Mt Blanc below the cols de la Seigne and di Chavannes.

2) Deffeyes. Alt. 2494m, 70 beds (18 winter). Tel: (0165) 884 239. C.A.I. Situated at the foot of the Rutor glacier.

3) Ruitor. Alt. 2030m, 45 beds. Tel: (0)4 79 06 92 12. Private. Situated on the French side of the frontier, west of the Testa del Rutor.

Valgrisenche

Scavarda. Marked on the maps but destroyed by fire.

4) Chalet de l'Epée. Alt. 2370m, 60 beds (6 winter). Tel: (0165) 97215. Private. Situated on the west facing side of the valley, above the head of the Lago di Beauregard. Open weekends only in September.

5) Mario Bezzi. Alt. 2284m, 40 beds. Tel: (0165) 97129. C.A.I. Situated near the head of the valley on the Alpage Vaudet.

On French side of frontier:

6) La Motte. Alt. 2080m, 36 beds. Tel: (0)4 79 09 51 30. Private. Recently renamed Refuge de l'Archeboc. Situated at the foot of the Col du Mont.

7) Du Monal. Alt. 1874m, 20 beds. Tel: (0)4 79 06 94 17. Private. Situated in the hamlet of the same name and reached over the Colle di Vaudet.

Val di Rhêmes

8) Benevolo. Alt. 2285m, 62 beds. Tel: (0165) 936 143. C.A.I. Situated near the head of the valley.

Valsavaranche

9) Vittorio Emanuele. Alt. 2730m, 96 beds. Tel: (0165) 95920. C.A.I. There are an old and a new refuge but meals are not provided at the old one. Situated on the west facing side of the valley, above Pont and at the foot of the Gran Paradis itself.

10) Federico Chabod. Alt. 2750m, 40 beds. Tel: (0165) 95574. Soc. Guide Valsavaranche. Situated on the same slope as the V. Emanuele but about $3^{1/2}$km north.

11) Citta di Chivasso. Alt. 2604m, 30 beds. Tel: (0124) 953150. C.A.I. Situated just north of the Col del Nivolet at the head of the Piano del Nivolet. Accessible by car from Ceresole Reale.

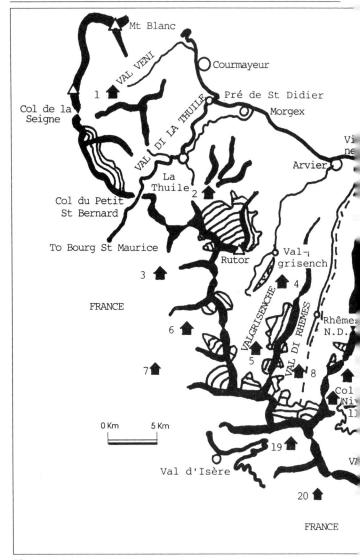

Map 3

The whole area covered by this guide showing the refuges 🏠 which provide food and two which are unguarded ⌂
The dashed line shows the limits of the National Park

To Col du Gd St Bernard

To Ivrea

Aosta

Aymavilles

Mt Emilius △

GRAUSON

Gmillian

Cogne

URTIER

Lillaz

Dondenaz 🏠 14

Champorcher

15 ⌂

Valnontey

13

Campiglia Soana

Ronco Canavese

17

18

Noasca

Pont Canavese

Locana

Ceresole DI Reale

Rosone LOCANA

ITALY

12) Savoia. Alt. 2532m, 50 beds. Tel: (0165) 94141. Private. Situated a little north of the Ref. Chivasso. Also accessible by car.

Valle di Cogne

13) Vittorio Sella. Alt. 2584m, 160 beds. Tel: (0165) 74310. C.A.I. Situated on the path to Col Lauson, west of the village of Valnontey.

Alpi Peradza. Being built at the top of the Urtier valley, at the foot of the Finestra di Champorcher.

Champorcher

14) Dondenaz. Alt. 2200m, 25 beds in 5 small rooms each with own wash room. There is overflow accommodation also. Tel: 0125 37 206. Private. Reached by road from Chateau Champorcher.

15) Miseran. Alt. 2582m. An unguarded refuge with cooking facilities. Situated by Lake Miseran some 3km west of Dondenaz.

Valle di Locana

16) Casa degli Alpinisti Chivassesi. Alt. 1667m, 50 beds. Tel: (0124) 95141. Situated in the bottom of the Orco valley, upstream of Ceresole Reale, near the road.

17) Pontese. Alt. 2200m, 40 beds. Tel: (0124) 800 186. Situated north of the Lago di Telecchio. It can be approached closely by road from the village of Rosone.

18) Pocchiola Meneghello. Alt. 2440m, 12 beds. Unguarded but always open. Cooking facilities. Just south of the dam of Lago di Valsoera, overlooking the lake.

In France:

19) Prariond. Alt. 2670m. Meals provided, 42 beds. Tel: (0)4 79 06 06 02. Parc National de la Vanoise. The other side of the Col de la Lhosa.

20) Carro. Alt. 2670m. Meals provided, 77 beds. Tel: (0)4 79 05 95 79. C.A.F. The other side of the Col du Carro.

Bivouacs

Only a few of these are of use to the walker and are mentioned in the text. Several can form the object of an outing but it must be emphasised that some are of difficult access *in the mountaineering sense*. These are:

Difficult of access - Balzola; Pol; Grappein

Moderately difficult of access - Borghi; Money; Martinotti; Gratton (all in Cogne region); Sberna (Valsavaranche)

SOME GENERAL INFORMATION

Geology

In the carboniferous and Permian periods, from about 300 to 250 million years ago, the region which is now the Graian Alps was made up of old, crystalline rocks, principally gneiss and micaschist. To the west of this was a low, partly submerged area of lakes and marshes. Erosion of the mountains and deposits of vegetable material in these lakes was to give black schists, coal and sandstone in later eras. In hollows which were not submerged, the erosion deposited sand and gravel, a process which continued until the whole region was more or less planar.

In the following period the Trias, the continents that were to become Europe and Africa, started to drift apart and a sea formed between them which geologists call the Tethys Sea, a very large area of water which perhaps stretched as far as Burma and which is not to be confused with the Mediterranean Sea. Thick deposits of sand formed on the beaches which were to become sandstone as the region evolved and, later, were a source of quartzite. Marine life produced deposits of calcium carbonate some 300 to 600m thick on the ocean floor. Some parts of the sea became partly separated from the remainder in a way that permitted extensive evaporation and ingress of further saline water to give very concentrated solutions. These eventually gave a deposit of a considerable bulk of evaporite of which gypsum (hydrated calcium sulphate) was a major constituent, together with salt and some dolomite. These deposits were to play an important part in future events.

At the end of the Trias, about 205 million years ago, there was sea to the south and east and land to the west and north. Geologists have named these regions the Piedmontese (submerged) and Brianconnaise (emerged). The continents continued to drift apart and the limestone layer formed in the Trias started to fracture by extension. There was further deposition in the sea both of animal skeleta and from erosion of the land to give mixtures of clay and chalk which were to metamorphose to schist, a major feature of the Graian Alps today. It is worth noting that an arm of the sea penetrated the Brianconnaise and that the sediments deposited there became major summits in the French Vanoise. Towards the end of this time, well into the Jurassic, the fracture of the submerged

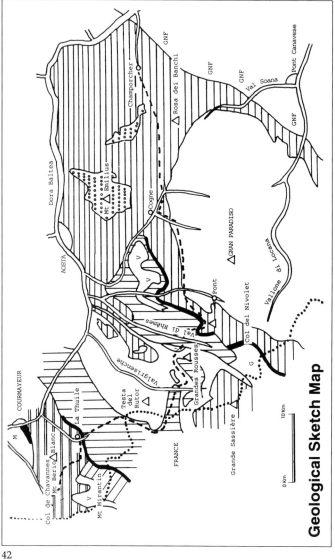

Geological Sketch Map

Simplified sketch map of the main types of rock to be found in the southern Valdotain and Gran Paradiso National Park. Some principal peaks are shown (△) as well as the line of the principal valleys (≈). In many of the valleys the floor is formed of alluvial deposits, which are not shown. There are also areas of ancient morain, which are not shown.

For further information see "Carte Géologique de la France à 1/250,000, No. 30, Annecy", published by BRGM, BP 6009, 45060 Orleans Cedex, France.

Symbol	Description
	Upthrusted ancient rocks of crustal origin and therefore crystalline
V	Volcanic rocks associated with the Carboniferous era
	Schists of the Tarentaise Flysch. These are lustrous, ie. they shine in the sun, but are of different origin to the Piedmontese lustrous schists
	Schists from the Carboniferous era
	The lustrous Piedmontese schists. These are differentiated according to the type of inclusion they contain. With one exception, these are not differentiated on the map. These ophiolites may be serpentines, gabbros or diabases
	Eclogitic micaschist of Mt. Emilius
M	A small complex region of which only gypsum is shown
G	A region mostly covered by glacier with several types of rock, including gypsum/dolomite to the west
GNF	A region of fine-grained Gneiss with schist further east
• • • • •	The French-Italian border
– – – –	Approximate line of the Via Alta 2
	Calschists of the Petit St Bernard
	Gypsum

43

strata was such that old crustal rock was exposed and was available for future mountain building. This change was accompanied by the submergence of the Brianconnaise. Strong sea currents prevented much deposition in this region but sedimentation continued in the Piedmontese part.

About 65 million years ago, at the beginning of the Tertiary era, the Tethys Sea had reached a width of between 600 and 1200km, but now the direction of continental drift reversed. Initially, the exposed old rocks slipped under the African plate and the relatively light sedementary strata were mostly swept along the surface though becoming piled more thickly in the process. Then, as the space available was reduced the rocks were concertina'd and metamorphosis was induced by the pressure and temperature increases engendered by these movements. By about 45 million years ago, the whole region had emerged from the sea and constituted a reasonably orderly "pile" of metamorphosed sediments which were to be completely overturned by the next tectonic phase, which is called the Alpine Folding. The approach of Europe and Africa continued but the space available for the original sediments became even more restricted, one tenth or one twentieth of that originally available, so that the folding of strata and the insertion of strata between each other became even more marked and the underlying crystalline rocks also became involved and were uplifted in their turn. The amount of uplifting seems to have been greatest in the Piedmontese region to the east and simple gravitational forces, aided by the underlying plastic gypsum which fulfilled the role of lubricant, resulted in the upper rocks in the Piedmontese sector sliding north-west into the Brianconnaise, on top of the rocks already present there. The gypsum was squeezed up to form whole mountains (between Courchevel and Pralognan) and is an important constituent of the Vanoise-Tarentaise region of France, but little is left of this material in the Gran Paradiso.

About 20 million years ago, uplifting of the whole region started, including the old, crystalline rocks of crustal origin. The increasing steepness of the ground meant that erosion became rapid and that in many places the underlying crystalline rocks were uncovered and came to form much of the higher relief. In the southern Valdotain and Gran Paradiso these were the summits of the Rutor and a much larger area around the Gran Paradiso itself. This uplift continues today at about 1.3mm per year. In between, the rocks were mostly schistose though with a variety of origins. Much of these have been given the name of the Piedmontese lustrous schists, following their marine origin in the east. It will be evident that during the long distance walks, many types of rock will be encountered and I will describe a traverse of the region from west to east in simple geological terms, with assistance from the geological sketch map.

We will start on the Colle di Chavannes, above the Vallon de la Lexe Blanche which is the extension of Val Veni. Looking south, the Vallone di Chavannes curves away below us on the left with Mt Bério Blanc beyond. This region is made up of what is called the Tarentaise Flysch. Flysch is material which has been eroded from mountains in course of folding and which itself has been caught up in the same folding process. The result is a schist with conglomerate included. This rock glistens in the sunlight due to the presence of flakes of mica and some good examples are to be seen by the VA2 path not far from the Colle di Chavannes. It is similar in appearance to, but is not of the same origin as, the Piedmontese lustrous schist. To the right from the col there is a ridge culminating in Mt Mirantin, below which there is a band of glacier. These rest on volcanic rocks. In addition, seams of gypsum bound the flysch which, with this aid, has slid over the strata to the north and has been partly covered by the Carboniferous rocks to the south.

Once past La Thuile, you are very quickly on these Carboniferous rocks, principally black schist and sandstone with a few anthracite measures. Looking ahead towards the Rutor, however, you see the ancient, crystalline crustal rocks and you are on or near these as you make your way around this mountain. These rocks also form the lower part of Valgrisenche though as you proceed towards the head of the valley the type of rock changes quickly and alternates between Carboniferous schist and crystalline rocks. The crest of the ridge of the Grandes Rousses is crystalline but as you drop into the Val di Rhêmes you again encounter Carboniferous country. The next ridge east is also Carboniferous and you cross this on the way to Valsavaranche, then descend onto a thin band of lustrous schist and quickly thereafter you enter the crystalline rocks of the dome of the Gran Paradiso. Not shown on the sketch map is a thin band of dolomite lying between schist and crystalline rocks. The VA2 crosses this country to Cogne where you encounter again the Piedmontese lustrous schists, which accompany you all the way to Champorcher.

On the other hand, if you follow the GTGP via the Col del Nivolet you stay with the crystalline rocks almost all the way.

Glaciation

Glaciation has been an immensely important influence on the aspect of this mountainous countryside. Following fault lines, the glaciers dug out the valleys, formed the intervening ridges and cirques and, where cirques overlapped, formed isolated "horns" such as the Cervin or Matterhorn. Alpine geologists recognise a series of ice ages of which the last three have left recognisable imprints. These, starting with the earliest, are called the Mindel, the Riss and the Würm glaciations, the latter finishing about 11,000 years ago. The effects of these three ice ages are seen differently on the French and Piedmontese sides of the Alpine Arc. On the French side, immense glaciers extended beyond Grenoble and only the Würm period is evident since this obliterated all traces of the earlier ice ages. These valleys contain many plain regions, evidence of glacial lakes and alluvial infilling. On the Piedmont side, however, the glaciers were much shorter and finished on the Piedmont plains. The principal glacier system followed the valley of the Dora Baltea from Courmayeur to Ivrea and was fed by the ice torrents of Mt Blanc, the Gran Paradiso and from the Italian side of the Pennine Alpine chain. These glaciers transported enormous quantities of material. At each ice age the glacier snout went a little less further with the result that the moraine arcs around Ivrea are visible for all three ice ages. The biggest was the Riss and this can be seen clearly from the motorway to the east as you drive on the section north of Ivrea, as a high, abrupt bank.

In the high mountains there are morains a little distance below the majority of the glaciers at present visible. These date from the quite recent past, from the mini ice age of the 17th and 18th centuries, the glaciers having been in retreat since this time. Prior to the 16th century, temperatures in the Alps were higher than now, and one wonders what significance this has for current theories of global warming?

FLORA

The summer show of flowers in the Alps is legendary and embellishes any expedition undertaken between the beginning of July and early September. The region has an abundant flora and many visitors like to have some idea of the names of the plants that they see. The lower slopes are full of flower early in the season and the colour climbs as the season advances. Many plants have to wait until the snow melts and it is often possible to observe around a still thick snowdrift a succession of flowers appearing each at a particular distance from its edge, dictated by how long the ground there has been clear of snow; a sort of time capsule, where different stages of the season coexist simultaneously. Blue gentians abound, the similar species *verna* and *bavarica* being in evidence most of the season, despite the significance of the name *verna* which means spring flowering. The trumpet gentian hereabouts is the species *kochii* and while locally very abundant, has a relatively short flowering period in each locality. There are many other blue flowered species and in addition there are one purple and two yellow gentians which may be seen. One is particularly tall, *gentiane jaune* or *Gentian lutea*, which can be up to 2m high. The roots are used to make an alcoholic drink called *gentiane*. The alpine pansy, *Viola calcarata,* is very common and has typically rich purple flowers with a yellow eye, though there are several colour variations about. A very striking flower common in the region is the yellow anemone, *Pulsatilla alpina subspecies apiifolia.* This is a large flower of 5cm diameter or more and of a lovely clear pale yellow. Where it grows, it can occur by the tens of thousands. There is a white form also, though this is less common. Both have striking seed heads. Less common, particularly in summer, when it will only be seen growing in rocks above 2000m altitude, is the pink primrose *Primula hirsuta* which glows at you from a shady niche. The similar *P. pedemontana* also grows in the region, and is particularly abundant above the Locana valley.

A very common family of flowers which is met at all altitudes are the campanulas with their bells of various colours but usually shades of blue. They tend to flower late in the season and so extend the time during which flowers are in evidence. There are a number of species related to the harebell but mostly one will remember the upright stems and hairy, hanging bells of *Campanula barbata* in colour varying from white to deep blue, the tall spikes of *C. spicata*, the curious tight yellow pokers of *C. thyrsoides*, the low mats of *C. cochliarifolia*, and more rarely, the blue-grey flowers of *C. cenisia* growing in rocky moraine where nothing much else can get a foothold, or *C. allionii* with its enormous blue bells competing in size with a garden grown Canterbury bell.

At higher altitudes the flora is less abundant but still striking. A white buttercup must be mentioned, *Ranunculus glacialis,* whose big flowers change in colour from white to pink after fertilisation. This plant seeks out places where there is plenty of moisture. Growing on the highest rocks and scree one may see *Androsace alpina* varying in colour from white to pink and the small flowers almost completely hiding the tight cushion of tiny leaves. Growing in stony scree one sometimes sees the pale purple *Thlaspi rotundifolia* with its strong scent of honey. The edelweiss grows hereabouts too, though it is a flower whose abundance varies widely from year to year. Also I have to mention the family of plants known as the *génépi* which are three species of *artemisia* with grey foliage and not very conspicuous yellow flowers in August. The plants grow at high altitude and the flowers have been coveted for centuries for their medicinal virtues. They are steeped in alcohol and the resulting highly flavoured liquor either added to hot water to make a herb tea, or sugar is added to make an aperitif. Most mountain people prepare *génépi*. It is said to have excellent restorative properties and many other beneficial effects.

Two magnificent lilies may also be observed. The orange lily flowers in June on rock ledges and is only found in a few inaccessible places. On the other hand, the Martagon lily is found in small groups all over, including woodland. It is tall and varies in colour from a dull pink to a really striking rose.

This list gives only a slight idea of the richness of the flora. A much better view can be obtained from the many books which have been written on the subject. Two handbooks which are small enough to fit in the rucksack are:

A. Huxley, *Mountain Flowers,* Blandford Press, Poole (1978).

C. Grey-Wilson and M. Blamey, *Alpine Flowers of Britain and Europe,* Harper Collins, London (1995 2nd Ed.)

These will assist the walker to identify many species on the spot.

Though be warned - it is a time-consuming process which can become a passion. A third book which is too big and too valuable for the rucksack but which contains beautiful photographs of most of the species of flower found in the region is:

E. Danesch and O. Danesch, *Le monde fascinant de la flore alpine*, Didier-Richard (1981).

FAUNA

The region has a number of indigenous mammals, large and small, many of which are not found in the UK and which may be seen during outings. The largest is the ibex, whose Italian name is stambecco and which the French call the bouquetin. It has very little fear of man and was easily hunted and so its numbers were much reduced, leading to the eventual creation of the Gran Paradiso National Park. They are also quite easy to photograph. The males have large and impressive curving horns with which they do battle in a rearing charge followed by clash of horns. The females are much smaller. The sexes graze apart for most of the year in herds, the young with the females.

Smaller, more attractive, but very difficult to approach is the

Via Alta 4: Chamois near the top of the Col Rosset

chamois with its short, backwards curved horns. They may be encountered in herds or as single animals but in all cases move quickly away from the intruder. They seem to enjoy sitting on snow patches on a hot summer's day.

The third mountain dweller that is likely to be seen and very much heard is the lovable marmot. This is reminiscent of a beaver in appearance though the tail is not so big. The colour varies from brown to golden. They live in deep burrows and when disturbed, run for cover but often pause for a good look at the cause of disturbance at the entrance to the burrow, standing on their hind legs to get a better view. When a predator, or human, appears in marmot country, distant animals emit a shrill whistling shriek to warn other marmots. Those nearby stay wisely quiet, though if they feel safe and out of sight can sometimes be seen peeping above the vegetation to observe what is going on. Their major predator is the golden eagle and the presence of this bird leads to their rapid disappearance underground. The best time to see marmots is in the early morning, and with care and patience they can be photographed. They hibernate from mid October to mid April, in burrows deep in the ground, when their heartbeat rate falls to two or three beats a minute. They awake every five days or so to perform their toilet.

Other wild animals which may be encountered high in the mountains are the ermine or stoat, the weasel, the fox whose presence causes high vocal activity among marmots, and the mountain hare.

Many species of bird live in the valleys and there are a few seen constantly high in the mountains. The raven with its hoarse croak and the chough with its sharp whistle echoing off the cliffsides are common. Birds of prey are omnipresent and several of the larger species are represented. The golden eagle breeds here and can be seen soaring high in the hills while buzzards fly frequently at the lower altitudes. The bearded vulture used to be present in the Gran Paradiso but has become extinct. However, it has been reintroduced further north and it has been suggested to me that it may be making a tentative return here. The kestrel will also be encountered and sometimes can be observed from above as they glide below a ridge. On the ground one may disturb ptarmigan or partridge. The alpine swift is impressive as it skims the ridges, sometimes almost passing between the legs of the walker.

Insects are represented principally and visibly by the butterflies and moths. These are attracted to high altitudes by the flowers and are a common sight. We have seen red admirals at 2500m, much higher than our books suggest is their limit. Their caterpillars will also be seen, some very gaudy and large. A common sight is a cloud of small butterflies collected around a wet patch in a path. These are called blues on account of the colour of the male though the female is a dull brown. Also audibly striking is the noise of grasshoppers which make an incredible din in the pastures on hot days. Flies are not really a problem, except on the pastures where animals are grazed. Nor is there anything to compete with the Scottish midge!

THE GRAN PARADISO NATIONAL PARK

The status of the region as a special area was first decreed in 1821 when a reserve was created to shelter the ibex. This majestic animal is not particularly afraid of man and is easy to kill with a rifle. It had long had a part in folk lore and superstition and was hunted not only for its meat but for other parts of the body which were believed to have medicinal values or to be capable of protecting the possessor from magic. There was also a belief that anyone who possessed a cross made from ibex horn would avoid a violent death.

From about 1836, Victor Emmanuel II, who became king of Savoie in 1848 and then king of the newly created state of Italy in 1860, started to create a royal hunting reserve which included the valleys of Champorcher, Cogne, Valsavaranche and Orco. He was successful in keeping the hunting much to himself and friends as he treated the local people very generously. He had something like 50 "gamekeepers", one of whose functions was to maintain the numbers of ibex. He hunted regularly between 1850 and 1876 and became known as "le Roi Chasseur" (the hunter King). He built, at his own expense, an extensive network of 350km of tracks, lodges and shelters, the tracks serving today as footpaths on the walks described.

His successors were much less keen on hunting and in 1919, King Victor Emmanuel III gave the reserve to the state to make a national park, whose statute was confirmed in 1922. A little later its size was increased to that of the present day, ie. 700sq km or 270sq miles. There were then something like 4000 ibex in the park. At the end of the Second World War these numbers had been drastically reduced by poaching, which was little hampered in the prevailing administrative chaos, and there were only about 400 remaining. The park has, however, since been intensively managed to provide these, and other animals, with a magnificent, wild but safe refuge. It is usual to see ibex as you pass through the park and you are also likely to see chamois. There are of course regulations which users of the park are expected to keep and these are posted at strategic points with multilingual text, including English.

The national park gets its name from the highest peak, the Gran Paradiso, but the origin of this name is uncertain. One rather nice explanation with an obvious religious origin bears repeating. At the head of Valnontey there is an enormous glacier which descends directly from the Gran Paradiso and which is called the Glacier of Tribolazione (tribulation). At the other side of the valley head there is the still high Torre del Gran San Pietro (tower of the Great St Pietro, 3692m) with attendant saints Andrea and Orso. With such a constellation of names it was not difficult to imagine that here was the eternal dwelling place, otherwise Paradise! However, others, more prosaically, hold that the name is a corruption of a much older name, the Grand Parei, which was often given to the highest point of a group of mountains. Or it may simply mean 'happy hunting ground' or hunting park from the Greek *paradeisos.*

FOOD AND DRINK

The food provided in restaurants is Italian in nature though very varied and there are several regional dishes which will be encountered, with the Orco valley having differences from the Valdotain. As a starter you may be offered Zuppa Valdostana which is a vegetable broth covered with bread upon which the local cheese, fontina, is melted. To the south-east a similar dish, Suepetta Cougnantse, may be offered. Everywhere, dishes based on polenta are offered. This is a sort of porridge made from ground maize and is very filling. It even has a song devoted to its consumption: *La Bella Polenta Cosi.* It can be incorporated into a meal in many ways; as a simple vegetable, or served with milk, or very tastily with cheese, which will be fontina in the Valdotain and salignon in the Orco valley.

The wines are also very pleasant and are produced at many centres in the Valdotain. The reds are good and I have found both Chambave and Pinot Noir excellent, and there are several others to choose from. In the Orco valley the wines are from the Canavese, and red Barbera and white Erbaluce di Caluso are reliable.

USING THE TELEPHONE IN ITALY

The Italian system is closely parallel to that used in the UK. Each district has its regional code, 0165 for the Valdotain, 0124 for the Orco (or Locana) valley, etc. If making a call within a district then this code is omitted. If making a call from outside Italy, then the code is used without the initial zero. To make a call from Italy to another country, the international code is 00, followed by the international code for the country desired: 44 for the UK, 33 for France or 41 for Switzerland for instance.

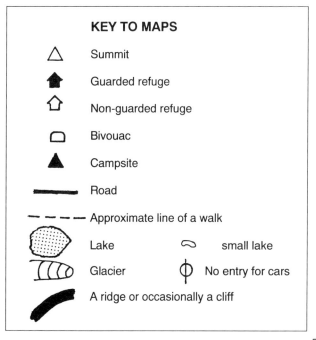

KEY TO MAPS

Summit

Guarded refuge

Non-guarded refuge

Bivouac

Campsite

Road

Approximate line of a walk

Lake   small lake

Glacier   No entry for cars

A ridge or occasionally a cliff

The Long Distance Walks

THE VIA ALTA 2, THE VIA ALTA 4, AND
THE GRAND TRAVERSE OF THE GRAN PARADISO

With such an array of prepared paths as existed in this region, it is not surprising to find that several long distance walks have been proposed. Historically, the first to be described seems to have been the Gran Traversata del Gran Paradiso or GTGP. This is described in Berutto's guide and goes west from Campiglia Soana, crossing a series of cols to run parallel with the Orco valley to the Col del Nivolet, whence it crosses to Valgrisenche via the Colle del Nivoletta and Colle Bassac Dere. The line taken is shown for this and the other walks on Map 4.

I do not know when this route originated. Berutto's guide is undated, but judging from the bibliography, is later than 1979 so that the walk must have been recognised before this.

Giglio and Orsières describe two long distance walks, the Via Alta 1 and the Via Alta 2 and variations. We will refer to these as the VA1 and VA2. The VA1 was inaugurated about 1978 and covers the northern Valdotain running parallel with the Italo-Swiss frontier, south of the big mountains. The waymarking for the VA2 was completed in 1981. We are only going to describe the VA2, which starts at Courmayeur and crosses cols from valley to valley going via La Thuile, Valgrisenche, Val di Rhêmes and Valsavaranche to Cogne then Champorcher. It nowhere coincides with the GTGP. There is plenty of accommodation in refuges or albergi. One section of the route crosses the Col di Planaval, a glacier col between La Thuile and Valgrisenche. It is probably inadvisable to direct British fellwalkers this way and I have provided an alternative, very attractive route through France to turn this obstacle. If you have glacier experience, then there is no reason why you should not use the Planaval col, but rope, ice axe and crampons are needed and it seems rather a lot to carry for the one short crossing.

Giglio and Orsières give many variations for the VA2 and these are marked on the 1:50,000 maps. On some of the 1:25,000 maps, however, these are given a new name, the Via Alta 4 or VA4. Waymarks are also found on the ground, a 4 in a black triangle with a yellow background (denoted here as $\triangle 4$, with $\triangle 2$ for the VA2 waymarking) so that one could safely assume that such a walk existed. Unfortunately, no documentation exists for this walk, which I found very puzzling. Eventually the tourist office at Aosta put me in touch with Signor Enrico Mauro who informed me that the VA4 was a dream! It had been proposed and waymarked but sections were found to be too difficult for a proportion of those who tried to use it, and it was decided not to advertise the route so as to minimise the likelihood of accidents. I will nevertheless describe the VA4 in full and emphasise the problems associated with the difficult bits. It is a splendid route which follows much the same direction as the VA2 but passes further south in the valleys and so goes much nearer the magnificent glacier scenery to be found there. Again, there is plenty of accommodation.

With three routes to choose from, it is necessary to give the reader some idea of their relative merits and disadvantages to enable you to choose which one suits you best. The VA2 is undoubtably the least technically difficult but as it often descends to lower parts of the valleys, the amount of ascent per stage is greater. The paths are everywhere good or excellent. The VA4 is technically difficult. There are four sections where there is some danger though these can all be missed out. Even then, this walk is more difficult than the VA2, though it passes through some marvellous places. The paths are not always good and the walker will have to expect to do some simple routefinding. On the other hand, the route stays generally much higher than the VA2 and so the amount of ascent is less. The part of the GTGP that I will describe has none of the dangers of the VA4 but is technically more difficult than the VA2, especially in its eastern part. The paths in the western part of the route are mostly good and follow old mule tracks. Unfortunately these are now much deteriorated in places, having been built some $1^1/2$ centuries ago. It is necessary at such points to pick your way among fallen blocks of various sizes which can make for slow progress. There are also odd bits where there are no paths at all. The route passes through what is often a wild, rocky chaos

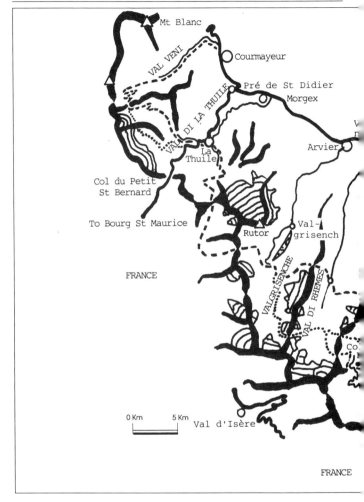

MAP 4.

Shows the general lines taken by the three long distance walks described. Via Alta 2 — — — — — , Via Alta 4 • • • • •, and the Grand Traverse of the Gran Paradiso — · — · — · · . Note that parts of the Via

Alta 2 & 4 coincide and only the line of the first is shown at these points.
The Grand Traverse starts in Valgrisenche and follows initially the Via
Alta 4. The most easterly part of the Grand Traverse is shown on the
map but is not described in the text.

below great rock walls which support the glaciers on the northern side of the ridge. Few other walkers will be encountered except at one or two popular places.

It will be evident from Map 4 that as the VA2 and VA4 run parallel and cross a series of valleys that run at right angles to the line of the walks, then it is possible to combine sections of the two walks by using connections along the valleys and so make circular expeditions of two, four or more days. Any section from valley to col can also be used for a day's outing, returning to base.

The walks will be described in the order VA2, VA4, then GTGP. Some shorter walks, some of which are parts of the long distance walks and some of which cover entirely new ground, will be described last.

The Via Alta 2

This walk is described starting from Courmayeur, though it can be done in either direction. It can of course also be started and ended at any desired centre between Courmayeur and Chateau Champorcher. The walk is summarised in the distance/height diagram where it will be seen that it is divided into six/primary stages, the stage points being low points on the walk. There is accommodation at all these places and there are also several refuges on the way so that the number of stages can be increased at will. The total distance is somewhat over 140km and total vertical ascent about 9000m depending on precise route and direction taken. The path is waymarked Δ2 though other marks will be encountered. Different features are given different names or variation of name on different maps and a glossary of these equivalent names is given below for the VA2, following the route as described.

Glossary of equivalent names

Veny,	Veni	Lex,	Lée
Porassy,	Porassey	Arpy,	Arpi
Aiguilles de l'Ermite,		Guglia dell'Hermite	
Rutor,	Ruitor	Revera,	Reveira
Grand Alpage,	Grand'Alp(e)	Forclaz,	Forciaz
San Grato,	St Grat	Plontaz,	Piontaz
Col de Fenêtre,	Finestra	Grolla,	Crolla
Feya,	Feyes	Lac Noire,	Nero
Eaux Rousses,	Eau Rousse		
Reale Casa di Caccia,		Reale Accampamento di Caccia.	

(Shown as c. d'Orvieilles on one map.)

Col Lauson,	Loson
Vallon Eaux Rouge,	Acque Rosse

VIA ALTA 2

Distance covered and height changes together with the standard times for the various sections, given for both directions of walking. Refuges are shown and the circles represent stage points and places with accommodation

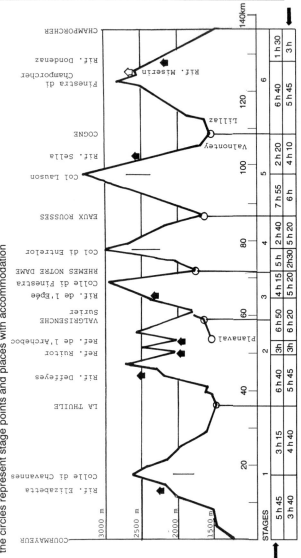

Mt Bério Blanc from the head of the Vallone di Chavannes

Stage 1:
COURMAYEUR TO LA THUILE

Grade: Mostly 1 or 2 but 3 then 4 on the ascent on the north side of the Colle di Chavannes.

Time needed: 9h. Height gain 1400m followed by 1160m descent. Map IGC 107. See Map 5 (p62).

Comment: A long day but mostly on road or tracks where the ground can be covered quickly. Indeed, timing is determined by distance as much as by ascent. The section can be broken at the Refuge Elizabetta. Views of the south wall of Mt Blanc.

Route: From the centre of Courmayeur, follow the ordinary road which goes to Entrèves but leave this and cross the river at the Ponte della Capre, just past La Saxe. The road now climbs steadily to the church of Notre Dame de Guerison, with the imposing chaos of the foot of the Brenva glacier on your right. Follow the road along the

61

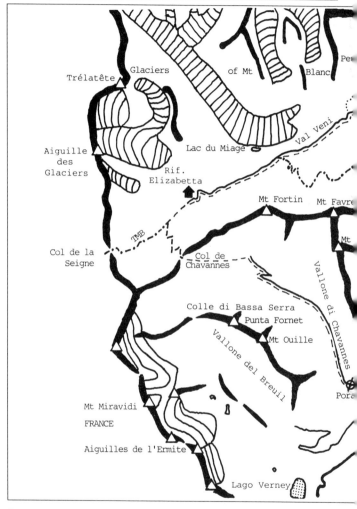

MAP 5.

Val Veni and Vallone di Chavannes. VA2 stage 1.
– – – – VA2; – · – · Tour of Mt. Blanc; ••• variation of VA2 via Peuterey.

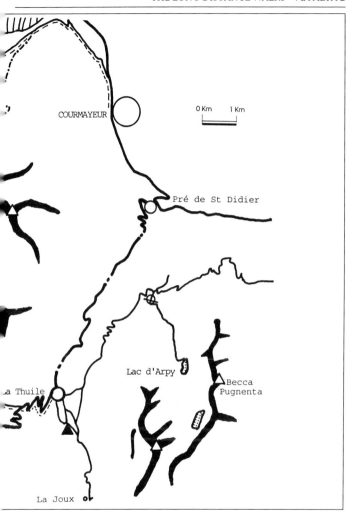

floor of the Val Veni. A pleasant alternative which avoids the traffic for a while is to go right at Purtud to the hamlet of Peuterey and take the path via Freiney (the bridge marked here does not exist) back to the road near Cantina della Visaille. There are two good bridges across the two arms of the river. The chaos ahead, closing the valley, marks the end of another big glacier, the Glacier de Miage. The road climbs to surmount this obstacle and then levels out in the Vallon de la Lex Blanche. On your right there is a high stony bank which is the edge of the glacier moraine. Above, over the top of the bank, is the curious tarn, the Lago del Miage, which is contained by the moraine on one side and the ice of the glacier on the other, and which it is possible to visit. Continue towards the Rif. Elizabetta which is reached up a series of zigzags.

To continue to the Colle di Chavannes keep left along what has long since become a track and then go left to climb the obvious path which zigzags up the valleyside. This relents near the summit then climbs steeply through rocks to the col where a magnificent panorama of the Massif de Mt Blanc can be enjoyed.

From the col, go east along a wide path above the Vallone di Chavannes which quickly turns into a track down the valley that links the various Chavannes hamlets. A detour can be made to include the ascent of Mt Fortin though this will add an hour to the day. As you descend the track, Mt Bério Blanc is ahead and the steep wall of Mt Ouille and Punta Fornet is on the right. The twin peaks of the Trélatête slowly disappear behind the head of the valley, while ahead are long views to the Rutor glacier and a preview of the start of tomorrow's walk.

You eventually emerge from the trough of the Chavannes valley at the ruined hamlet of Porassey where the track becomes surfaced. The road over the Col du Petit St Bernard is visible across the main valley. This is reached using the road from Porassey and is followed to La Thuile.

Lakes Leità, Rosset and Trebecchi from below Punta Basei.
Grand Nomenon behind (VA4)

Climbing névé towards the Colle del Nivoletta, Punta Basei behind. (VA4)

The ice falls on the north east side of the Gran Paradiso from the Herbetet chalets. (VA4)

Valgrisenche and Lago di Beauregard from near Verconey

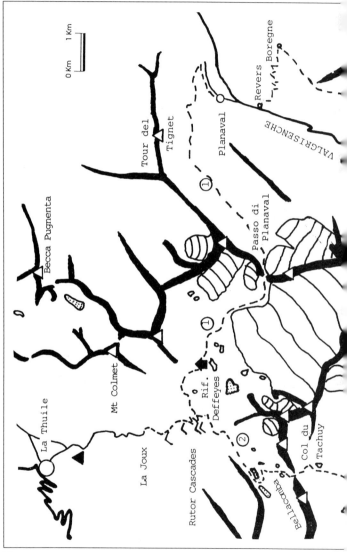

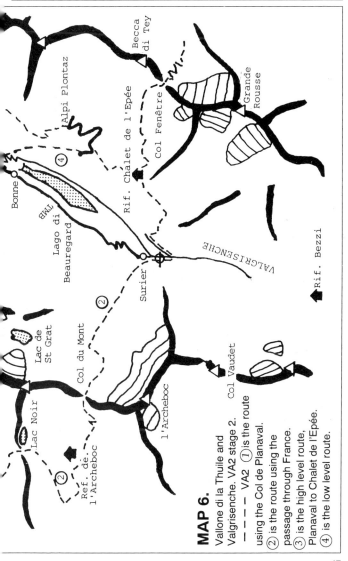

MAP 6.

Vallone di la Thuile and Valgrisenche. VA2 stage 2.

– – – VA2 ① is the route using the Col de Planaval.

② is the route using the passage through France.

③ is the high level route, Planaval to Chalet de l'Epée.

④ is the low level route.

Stage 2:
LA THUILE TO VALGRISENCHE

Grade: 3 with some 4. See Map 6 (p66).

Comment: The "official" route over the Planaval col is not
               described. For those wishing to do this, it may be
               possible to hire a guide and crampons at La Thuile,
               though it would have to be arranged that the guide
               took the crampons back for you. Individual guides
               can be contacted via the tourist office or ring the
               Cooperativa Interguide on 44448.

The route passes the magnificent Rutor cascades. The British
mountaineer William Mathers in 1868 commented that this walk
was one of the most beautiful in the Alps. The Lagi di Bellacomba,
on the route to be described, are also well worth a visit and the view
of the Rutor from the Col du Tachuy is magnificent.

*There is also an old tale connected with the Rutor glacier. Legend has
it that the waste of the ruitor glacier was not always covered with ice but
in times long past was a lush pasture owned by a rich but hard farmer. One
day Charity came to his door disguised as a beggar and asked for a drink of
milk from the enormous cauldron in which the yield of the day's milking
had been stored. The farmer refused but the beggar persisted until, in a rage,
the farmer told his workers to overturn the cauldron to show the beggar that
he would not listen to her entreaties. The milk ran over the pastures in little
streams spreading its whiteness far and wide. The farmer gloated over the
beggar but Charity threw back her hocd and cried "Your iniquity has called
the anger of God on this earth." She looked upon the pastures flooded with
milk and said sadly "See how the fields whiten in the distance", and,
looking to the sky, "The clouds are appearing already." The rich farmer also
looked up to see enormous storm clouds advancing, blotting out the light.
When he looked down again, the beggar had disappeared but the phrase
"See how the fields whiten in the distance" still rang in his ears. He woke
early in the morning to find that indeed all the pastures were covered in
snow. The snow fell continuously, day and night, covering, then burying
the rich man and all his land and possessions. Only the snow remains and
will remain until the end of the world.*

Route through France:

Time needed: 16¹/₂h. The stage will therefore need to be broken by staying at one of the French refuges, the Ruitor or the Archeboc. The stage ends at the Rifugio de l'Epée on the eastern wall of Valgrisenche. There is 2800m of ascent and 1900m of descent.

Because this route covers the frontier region, several maps are needed to show it all. Of the 1:25,000 maps, none shows the Lagi di Bellacomba but IGC Nos.102 and 107 plus the French IGN TOP25 No.3532ET (Les Arcs & La Plagne) cover the rest. In the 1:50,000 series, the two French Didier & Richard maps Nos.8 & 11 cover almost the whole walk, except the last bit to the Chalet de l'Epée. Italian IGC No.3 covers the whole but in less detail.

Route: Follow the road from La Thuile to La Joux where there is a restaurant and car park. Take a path on the left which takes you by the Rutor cascades. The latter part of the climb to the top of the third cascade is steep but eventually reaches level ground where a bridge allows you to cross the stream and continue to the right towards the Lagi di Bellacomba. There are two lakes and you pass the first on its right, then cross to the left between the lakes and make a steep traversing climb left up the hillside ahead on a narrow path. This brings you to a small lake which is passed on its right, then up a steep short wall to a second lake which is passed on its left. The path now climbs steadily towards the Col du Tachuy which is well over on the right (facing the hillside) and is reached without difficulty, though the path may be partly obscured by *névé*. The descent from the col is steep and then a rough path takes you down to the Lac du Petit and scrambles among blocks on its right. The path continues past the lake and then gradually descends the hillside on the right to arrive at a little green oasis among big boulders. Cross the stream (avoid a false path which does not cross) and follow the path down to the Refuge Ruitor.

From the refuge, cross the plain to a ruined hamlet and take the path which climbs the hillside ahead, tending a little to the right. Less steep ground is reached and is crossed keeping close to the side of the Monseti ridge. A little col will be seen up slabs on the right where a narrow path takes you up onto the crest of the ridge with the Monseti Lac Noire a little lower on the left. Follow a path which traverses away from the head of the lake to the top of a shallow gully which is descended to a path which traverses right again and takes you down into the Vallon du Mercuel to the hamlet of Le Bochet and a track which is followed left to the refuge at La Motte (Ref. de l'Archeboc).

It is possible to make straight for the refuge from the foot of the gully, with some trace of path to help.

From the refuge a path climbs to the right up the hillside behind to the Col du Mont which is reached without difficulty. Descend more or less directly, keeping a little right and passing a ruined building not marked on the maps. The path eventually zigzags down a steep ridge then traverses left to a bridge and climbs a little, to near the Alp Revera Basse and so to a track which is followed to Grand Alpage, where it is possible to descend almost directly to cut out a big hairpin and so arrive at the hamlet of Surier. One could in fact walk to the village of Valgrisenche from here and continue the route by following the Boregne - Verconey - Epée path, but much saving of distance and ascent is made by continuing directly to the Chalet de l'Epée. Descend the road from Surier, cross the river and turn right on a road which quickly becomes a track. Follow this south for a short distance up to a junction, where you turn sharp left. Follow the track, which climbs steadily until a notice and path are seen on the right. It is possible to continue on the track to the Chalet de l'Epée but it is pleasanter to take the path. This zigzags up through open larch woods which are distinguished by being a protected zone because of some very aged trees, which are estimated to be five centuries old. You emerge onto open hillside and the path levels out making for the Alp du Mont Forclaz, which is reached across one of two bridges. Go past the buildings to the most northerly one where a path makes a climbing traverse of the hillside behind (there is another notice) and brings you to a level, rocky chaos which the path crosses in meanders to join a track, which is not on my 1:25,000 map. Just across the track are the buildings of the Alp de l'Epée and the refuge is visible on the right as a long, low building higher up the hillside. Follow the track to reach this. Note that the position of the refuge on the map is erroneous. Note also that this route through the larches is not officially the VA2 and there are no waymarks.

Stage 3:
VALGRISENCHE TO RHÊMES NOTRE DAME

Grade:	3 with some sections at 4.
Map:	IGC 102.
Comment:	There are several starting points for this section: the Chalet de l'Epée if using the French variant for the previous section, or if starting in Valgrisenche then Valgrisenche village or Planaval. Each uses different routes initially, but converge at the Chalet de l'Epée.

From Valgrisenche village:
Time needed: 3¹/₄h to Chalet de l'Epée. See Map 6 (p66)

Route: Go south from the village centre and keep left by the river until a bridge is reached which crosses the river near a chapel. There are new buildings here which seems to have obliterated the path but go right and follow the river to a low wall and climb left on a path, indistinct at first, which takes you into the woods. You take to the road at the second hairpin bend and follow this to waymarks on the left (the map is inaccurate here) and take to the woods again. You see the road once more then climb steeply through pleasant woodland to an altitude of about 2100m where the angle eases and the woods become more open. At Benevy you reach open hillside and climb a little, tending leftwards, then traverse to the Alpi le Bois where a track takes you across the river. It is possible to cut the next hairpin bend on a path to the left but you quickly regain the track and climb towards some ruined chalets. You will see a signpost a little up the

Valgrisenche and the Grande Rousse from Col Vaudet

hillside on the right, too far away to read. Pass below this and reach a path which goes back on the right, which you follow, passing by this signpost. The path now takes you past a series of little combes then climbs to a shoulder and continues less steeply to a level place from whose edge you can see the refuge, quite close on the left with the buildings of the Alpage d'Epée below on your right.

Note that if the building at the start of the path obstructs the way in future years then it will be necessary to follow the road to below the dam of the Lago di Beauregard and take to the path after the second hairpin.

From Planaval:

Time needed: 6^{1}/$_{2}$h to Chalet de l'Epée. If following the valley to Valgrisenche village, allow about 1h plus time for previous section. See Map 6 (p66)

Route: Evidently, this can be done simply by walking up the valley from Planaval to Valgrisenche village to the start of the previous route. There is, however, a much pleasanter though longer route which makes an undulating traverse along the eastern side of the valley with good views, particularly of the Rutor group and its glaciers.

Follow the road from Planaval to the main road and continue to the side road to the hamlet of Revers. It is worth pausing on the bridge. There are several good examples of roches moutonnées around, including an enormous one on the edge of the hamlet on which a house is being built. A track leaves the rear of the hamlet and makes for the hillside where it turns sharply right. Follow this for a little way until you see a wooden signpost on the left pointing up the hill with the legend Becca di Tos, Boregne. The start of the path is not obvious but is in the direction of the arrow and behind the plane of the signpost. The path quickly becomes well established and leads steeply up through dense forest. Waymarks are red and white here but change to red only as you get higher. The VA2 marking is not used.

Eventually you start to make a climbing traverse north and the path becomes a veritable drove road. You come to the edge of pasture where the path is overgrown. Keep left at first then cross right to a little tree covered knoll where the path is again evident. A few metres further on you are in sight of the buildings of the Alpi Boregne. The Matterhorn makes a fine sight to the north. Pass the chalets on the right and find an excellent mule track which takes you on a gentle climbing traverse through open woods to the right. Follow this up to its summit at about 2200m then descend quickly at first then gently through woods to the chalets of the Alpi di Verconey d'en haut. The path passes behind two large boulders to reach a track and fades out as it does so. This is of no great consequence if going in the direction described, but if you are going the other way is a nuisance. There is a wooden signpost by the track, in front of the boulders. Find this then pass behind the boulders to pick up the path.

At the Alp of Verconey d'en haut you reach a track which has recently been pushed further up the hillside and has obliterated what previously appears to have been the path. Follow this new track up the hillside and past four hairpin bends, then up to the next bends where a track will be seen which goes off on the right to some waterworks buildings. Go behind these and climb a little on a path then descend through the edge of woods to a point where there is a crossroads of paths and some more waterworks buildings. Continue south and climb gently, then more steeply to the ruins at Grolla, then very steeply on a ridge to the left, to below some cliffs, where you go right and take a path which traverses towards an obvious square cairn at about 2400m altitude. Follow the path across level meadow and cross a stream to join a new track which descends to near-by Alpi Plontaz. From here you follow a track down in big zigzags and round to the path junction and signpost already mentioned for the route from Valgrisenche village. Take the path left and follow the route already described.

From the Chalet de l'Epée:

Time needed: From chalet to Rhêmes Notre Dame $4^{1/}4$h. The route is on Map 7

Route: Follow a track which climbs from the south side of the refuge and follows the line of the river to bring you to the bottom of a flat combe where the track peters out. A path reappears after a short distance which is indistinct at first but makes for the left-hand wall of the combe with the imposingly steep sided Becca di Tey always ahead. Eventually you start to zigzag up the steep scree below the mountain, making right and aiming for the gap in the crest above, which is further to the right. This is the Colle di Finestra, the climb being very steep for the last few metres. The top is quite spacious, with a view indicator. The ground ahead drops away disconcertingly steeply but a good path zigzags down the steep grass slopes without any real difficulty. You are in a gully with high craggy sides and scree slopes which are avoided as far as possible. The gully narrows towards its foot and the path keeps to the right wall to emerge into an open combe. The path below has been covered by stones brought down by recent floods and is a little difficult to follow but keep right at first, then cross over to the left and so to the buildings at Alp Torrent which have been built so as to blend into the mountainside. The path now traverses left above the ravine of the Torrent stream onto open hillside overlooking Val di Rhêmes, and descends to the road in steady zigzags.

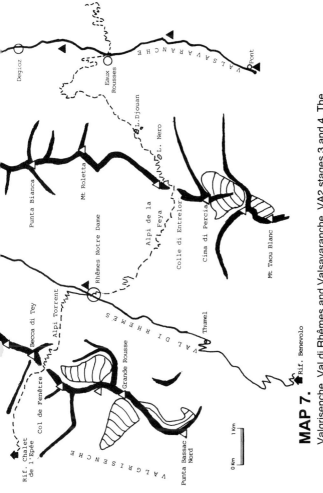

MAP 7.

Valgrisenche, Val di Rhêmes and Valsavaranche. VA2 stages 3 and 4. The various routes to the Chalet de l'Epée are shown on map 6. – – – – VA2.

Stage 4:
RHÊMES NOTRE DAME TO EAUX ROUSSES

Grade: 3 with a short section at 4.

Time needed: 7h 40m. This is the only stage where there is no intermediate accommodation. Map IGC No.102. Height gain 1280m, descent 1330m. Route shown on Map 7 (p75).

Comment: A long but pleasant crossing via the Col di Entrelor (3007m) which passes some attractive spots where one might wish to linger.

Route: Pass through the hamlet of Breuil-Rhêmes Notre Dame following the signposts to the Col di Entrelor. This takes you across the river to the tourist office. There is a sculpture of a bearded vulture and, just behind, a narrow path climbs above the road. This zigzags up through forest and makes height steadily to leave the forest by a cross at 2097m. There is one path junction where a branch goes left and is signposted to the Colle di Sort (a col we are advised to avoid by Janet Adam-Smith) whereas you traverse right. You will also meet another path which climbs from below and joins on the right, but this causes no problem as your way is always upwards.

The ground now becomes much less steep and you wander through pleasant alps with the Chalets d'Entrelor over on the right; the branch of the path marked as passing through the chalets seems not to be used. A steeper climb leads to the buildings at the Alp Plan de la Feya where there is a water supply. The path now climbs a shallow gully with paths leaving on the right which are of no use to you. Then you enter a zone of scree below a rock wall up which the path makes a climbing traverse at first then starts to zigzag up more steeply, aiming for a gully to the left of a blade of rock. A little scramble up the gully, then to the right, brings you onto an exposed ridge which in fact is the top of the blade of rock. One is quickly past the exposure and further scree takes you to the now near col which is spacious and a good place for a pause and refreshment.

The descent path is quite a contrast to the one you have just used and I suspect owes its good state to the hunter king. It descends

Rhêmes Notre Dame, Bruil village

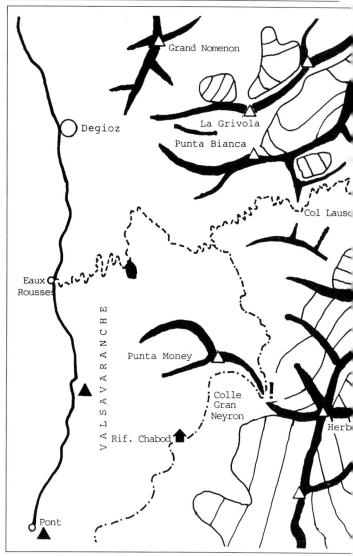

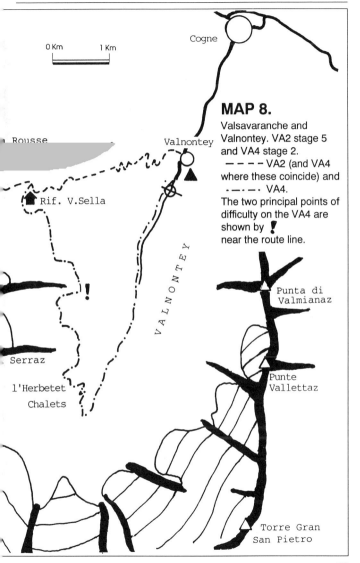

MAP 8.

Valsavaranche and Valnontey. VA2 stage 5 and VA4 stage 2.
– – – – VA2 (and VA4 where these coincide) and
·—·—· VA4.
The two principal points of difficulty on the VA4 are shown by ❗ near the route line.

easily to the artificial Lago Nero, which was thronged with picnickers when I passed, and continues past the pretty Lago Djouan to traverse above the Torrente Nampie - reminiscent of the end of the previous stage - and turns the end of the ridge above to head in the direction of the Reale Casa di Caccia at 2190m. This royal hunting lodge looks as if it might have seen better days though in 1860 it is unlikely that even a king had his own electricity generating turbine. Go through the buildings and continue horizontally for a while, then turn downhill as shown on the map, but follow the path left after a short descent to pass a low building on its left which is not shown on the map. Go around a fenced off field and take the steady descent to Eaux Rousses. There is a path junction signposted to Creton and lower down a less evident junction where you can go directly, or less so, to Eaux Rousses, where you arrive essentially in the hotel grounds.

Stage 5:
EAUX ROUSSES TO COGNE

Grade:	3 on lower slopes, 4 on upper.
Time needed:	10$^{1/}$4h but can be broken at Rif. Vittorio Sella. Maps IGC Nos.102 and 101. Height gain 1650m and descent 1800m. See Map 8 (p78)
Comment:	A varied route which reaches the highest point of the walk, Col Lauson, at 3296m. The approach paths to the col are everywhere excellent though the col itself is not easy, being steep, slippery and somewhat exposed.

Route: Cross the river at Eaux Rousses and climb through open fields on a zigzag path. This soon enters the forest and becomes a velvet surface of pine needles which conducts you pleasantly upwards. A long traverse north follows to open terrain at Levionaz d'en bas where there is a cabin devoted to research in the national park. The path turns right, around the end of a ridge and enters the upper part of the valley of the Torrente Levionaz and follows the river along level pastures. You quickly take to the valley side to

*Morning sun on the mountains on the east side of Valnontey,
from above the Rif. V. Sella*

make altitude, then swing left across the river to climb more steeply
to a path junction at the end of a steep ridge. The right branch is part
of the VA4, leading to the Colle di Grand Nomenon. A notice warns
you that what you are about to undertake is not easy, though,
strangely, no comment is made about the much more difficult
Nomenon col. You enter a steep, upper valley, dominated by the
sombre wall of the Punta Bianca, and zigzag interminably up steep
scree to below the col. The last part of the climb goes right, and is
steep and slippery, needing care and effort. The col is quite roomy
and a good place for a halt. The path on the other side crosses the
head of a gully. This section is exposed and has been provided with
a chain handrail for security. Several of the anchorage points had
broken away when I was there, no doubt because of the weight of
the winter's snow, and the chain rather got in the way. It leads to a
sort of false top to the col and helps to surmount this last obstacle
before you make a steep descent on scree. This leads down to a good
path which crosses a bowl where there may be *névé*, then swings
down steadily to the Rif. V. Sella. This part of the path, above the

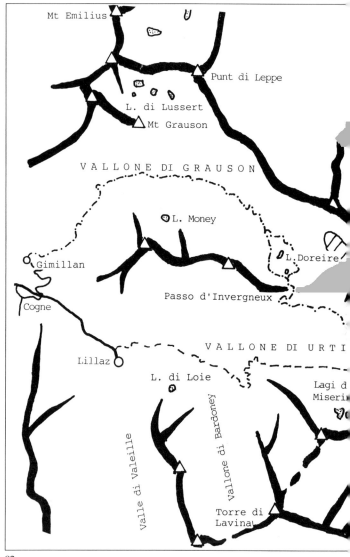

MAP 9.

Grauson, Urtier and Champorcher valleys.
VA2 stage 6 and VA4 stage 1. VA2 is shown – – – – –
and VA4 – · — · — except where the two
coincide, in which case the VA2 marking is used.

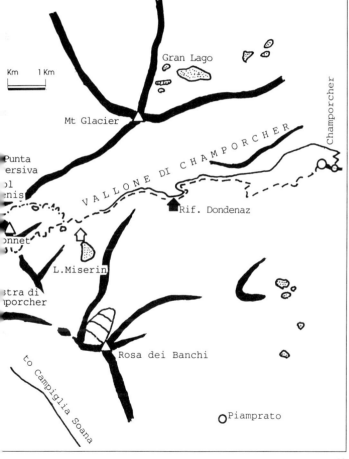

refuge, is renowned for its herds of ibex.

To continue down from the refuge, follow the good path which runs parallel with the Torrente Lauson and descend in zigzags and traverses to Valnontey, passing as you do beside the garden Paradisia. From Valnontey, Cogne is reached either by path on one side of the river, or by road on the other.

Stage 6:
COGNE TO CHATEAU CHAMPORCHER

Grade:	2 though long, with a stiff climb over the Finestra di Champorcher.
Time needed:	9h. Map: IGC No.101. Height gain 1340m and descent 1420m. The route is on Map 9 (p82).
Comment:	This is a long stage which can be broken by staying at the Rif. Dondenaz and/or shortened by using the bus service Valnontey-Cogne and Cogne-Lillaz.

Route: Walk or bus from Cogne to Lillaz. Just as you enter Lillaz a road goes off left and climbs the hillside, rising quickly above the village. Follow this until a wooden bridge across a big water pipe allows you to gain a path which continues to climb, crosses meadows past some chalets and then levels out until a bridge across the river is reached, just below a small dam. None of the maps in my possession depicts this part of the route with any accuracy. The path now quickly enters the forest, through which it climbs steeply to get above the gorge of the Torrente Bardoney. The forest is open and pleasant, consisting principally of larch and Arolla pine. The latter has its needles in bunches of five and blueish cones which are the favourite food of the nutcracker, a bird you are also likely to see hereabouts. Eventually you reach a pleasant glade at the entrance to the Bardoney valley where a path goes right to the hamlet of Bardoney. You take the left fork.

The path crosses two new bridges then climbs again past a cabin and emerges from the forest on open slopes above the Urtier. A gentle climb follows past junctions right to the Vallon Eaux Rouge and the Lagi di Miserino to descend slightly to a track not far below

Alpi Peradza where one day a rifugio may be built. Follow the track past the buildings and incline left over a bridge. Up on the slope on your left is a V shaped bank and wall constructed for protection against winter avalanches. The path threads its way among these and makes long zigzags up the steep scree slope ahead to reach the Finestra di Champorcher (2828m). This is unfortunately adorned by an electricity pylon and a shelter which is both "pericoloso" and disgustingly littered. You leave the national park at this point and descend using a wide path which traverses the left-hand wall of the valley ahead. This quickly turns into a well made mule track which zigzags its way easily down, across a clapper bridge and then joins a track below Lago Nero which takes you gently down to Dondenaz where the refuge is seen only at the last moment. It is possible to make a deviation to manmade Lago Miserin from here, or there is a narrow path which will take you directly to the lake from the Finestra di Champorcher.

Below Dondenaz, the track crosses the river and continues to Champorcher, eventually becoming a road. It appears to be possible to take a path down through the forest but this is used as a ski route and I suspect will be rather steep and badly graded - ski routes and paths are never really compatible!

Note that red and blue waymarks will also be found on this route.

The Via Alta 4

This walk is described starting at Champorcher since this means that the via ferrata of the Colle di Grand Nomenon is ascended rather than descended. It can, however, be done in either direction and started or ended at any desired centre. The walk is summarised in the distance/ height diagram where it will be seen that it is divided into six primary stages which are not much different from those of the VA2. There is plenty of accommodation along the route and the number of stages can be increased as desired. The total distance is about 170km and the total vertical ascent around 9900m depending on the precise route taken. The path is waymarked Δ4 though other waymarks will be encountered. As mentioned earlier, there are four places which may be too difficult for some parties. These are the section Valnontey - Herbetet chalets - Rif. V. Sella, the ascent to the Colle di Grand Nomenon, and two points between the Colle di Bassa Sera and the Colle di Chavannes. In each case as precise a description as possible of the problem will be given and alternative routes outlined.

Glossary of equivalent names

Col des Hevergnes,	Passo d'Invergneux
Piano di Ressello,	Recelloz
Penna Ceinlla,	Sengia
Col Lauson,	Loson
Lago Leità,	Leytaz
Vaudelaz,	Vaudala
Laghi di Trebecchi,	lac des Trois Becs
Gliarettaz,	Gliairettaz
M. Lechand,	Lechaud

Via Alta 4.

Distance covered and height changes together with the standard times for the various sections, given for both directions of walking. Refuges are shown 🔺 and the circles represent stage points and places with accommodation. The bars ╱ show four difficult sections.

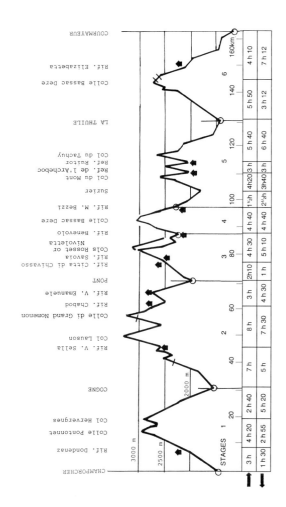

87

Stage 1:
CHAMPORCHER TO COGNE

Grade: 3 with short sections of 4. A long day.

Time needed: 10h. Ascent 1655m, descent 1630m. The route is on Map 9 (p82). The full stage is only depicted on the 1:50,000 maps; part is on IGC No.101.

Comment: This route crosses two high cols which makes it a more demanding walk than the VA2 variation. It can be broken at the Rifugio Dondenaz or the unguarded Rif. Miseran.

Route: One can start at the hamlet of Chardonney and climb a ski piste, though many may prefer to keep away from the uplift and follow the road which goes north from the hamlet of Chateau. This zigzags steeply up the hillside, becomes a track and climbs gently to the hamlet of Dondenaz. It is indeed possible to drive to this point. The Rif. Dondenaz is some 500m further along a track and is visible across the valley to the south, being the highest building with a flag flying. From the refuge, continue along the track as far as the third signpost, which directs you to the Colle di Pontonnet. Descend immediately right from the track, cross the river and follow a path which is a little vague at first but which quickly becomes well defined and zigzags up a scree slope ahead. The slope eases near the first Lago di Pontonnet, passes this on its right and joins a well preserved mule track where you go left. The track zigzags to the Col di Fenis but before you actually get there another goes left and makes for the Colle di Pontonnet (2897m), which like the Finestra di Champorcher is adorned with a pylon and a pericoloso shelter. There is an excellent view north-east between two near-by peaks of the Monte Rosa group. Ahead, the path descends on the left to the Lagi di Pontonnet, a large tarn with a satellite, over scree dotted with scree plants in August and the biggest concentration of pink *Androsace alpina* that I have ever seen. Pass the lake over big boulders at first and on its left, then traverse grass slopes until the path turns left and plunges steeply down a hillside to a small chalet. The maps are a little confusing here as the chalet is new and is not marked. The Alpi Ponton and Lago di Ponton are below you, but

The descent of the Grauson valley, above Ecloseur. The peak is the Grivola

you do not descend to these. The path follows a ridge and is marked O7c on the ground but follows approximately the line marked O8 on my large scale map, which goes to the track by the chalet. Follow the track to the right for a short way and then strike off right on a path which climbs fairly gently at first over grassy slopes. The path disappears on a level area then starts to climb more seriously in a series of steps crossing steeper and steeper grass slopes and finally, scree, to the Col des Hevergnes (2905m), a roomy spot with superb views to the south of the Gran Paradiso and the Lagi di Miserino in their rocky combe. The far side of this col is again well covered with scree flora, and the grass slopes on the ascent carry abundant edelweiss.

On looking north from the col a small lake can be seen below which is not named on the map. Descend easy slopes to the left of this and then follow a depression above cliffs on the right to arrive at Lago Doreire.* Paths parallel with the Torrente Grauson are then followed down the Grauson valley, crossing the stream to its north

---

* There are more difficult alternative descents to the right which are marked on some of the Italian maps.

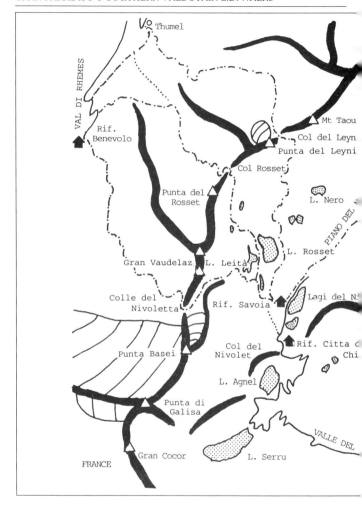

MAP 10.

The region around the heads of the valleys Orco (Locana),
Valsavaranche (Piano del Nivolet branch), and Val di Rhêmes. VA4
stages 2 and 3. Part of stage 2 is shown on map 8. VA4 is —·—·—,

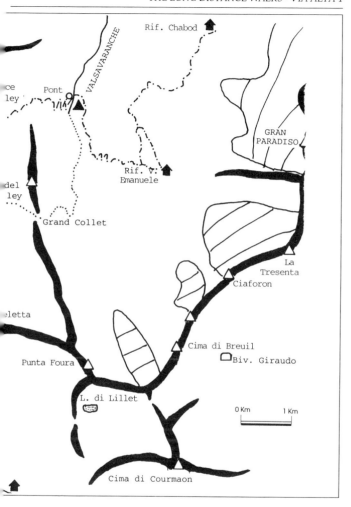

including the three possible routes between the Colle del Nivolet and Val di Rhêmes.

Variants are shown as • • • • •

side near Alpi Pralognan. Continue to a bridge just above Alpi Grauson (Vieux) which is crossed to bring you down to a flat pasture.

A much better path now takes you down the valley keeping up above the left bank of the stream and as the valley curves left, bringing the Grivola into view. The path takes a sudden plunge through some cliffs with an attractive waterfall on the right and descends gently to the chalets at Ecloseur. A bridge takes you across the river again and you climb a little to traverse out of the valley onto pastures which you descend to Gimilan (*pron.* "jeemilan"). From here it is best to follow the road to Cogne, or there is a bus service. There are alberghi at Gimilan, at Cogne and at Valnontey, and campsites at the latter.

Two Italian walkers whom I met on the Col de Hevergnes had used a route past Lago Money which is apparently waymarked, at least in part, which could make a pleasant alternative.

Stage 2:
COGNE TO PONT

Grade:	Up to 4 with two sections at 4M.
Time needed:	17$^{1/2}$h with a total of 2850m ascent and 2400m of descent. This is a long stage and it is recommended that one night is spent at the Rif. V. Sella and one at Rif. Chabod. Map IGC 101. Route shown on Map 8 (p74) with the last short part on Map 10 (p90) Chabod to Pont.
Comment:	This is one of the two most difficult stages of the VA4 but one which passes through magnificent scenery. There are three chained sections, two of which are difficult but can be avoided and one which cannot be avoided but is straightforward. This stage will be described in sections. It is advisable to book the two refuges well in advance, particularly Rif. Chabod.

Route:

First section: Cogne to Rif. V. Sella: 7h for 1350m ascent and 275m descent. From Cogne walk to Valnontey using either path or road. If using the path, cross the river at Valnontey and follow road then track south along the Valnontey valley to the hamlet of Valmianaz. Continue on the same side of the river to the Pont de l'Erfaulet on a track which is much damaged by floods. Do not cross the river just after Valmianaz as marked on my IGC map as this section of path marked as VA4 has been cut by a rockfall. Cross the river at Erfaulet, pass big blocks, climb through woods then follow a series of zigzags on open hillside which gain height rapidly and arrive at the Herbetet chalet at 2435m. Up to this point you are on a popular walk and many parties reach this place where there is a supply of drinking water.

The VA4 path continues north, traversing past one or two exposed places to the pleasant platform of the Pian di Ressello where a large notice warns picnickers to behave! You now drop gradually into the steep V of the stream, the Rio Gran Val, and cross the stream on some big blocks in its bed. Then make a climbing traverse of the opposite side of the gully on a narrow path which becomes increasingly exposed. The path traverses the slopes of the Bec du Vallon where there are occasional passages of scrambling and in places the need to step over ribs of rock which cut the path. The path disappears for a short section and is bridged by planks protected by a chain handrail. Some walkers will find this section quite frightening, and, if in doubt, should use the direct path up to the refuge from Valnontey, ie. the VA2 route.

Once past this point the path suddenly widens to an ample mule track, near the Welsh sounding Penna Ceinlla, and you have a relaxing walk past the Lago di Lauson and down to the Rif. Sella across a bridge. This spot is usually thronged with picknickers during the day but quietens down at night.

Second section: Rif. V. Sella to Rif. Chabod: 8h for 1350m of ascent and 1190m of descent. From the refuge follow a narrow path along the river in the direction of Col Lauson and reach the well defined main path after about ³/₄km.

This is followed easily and is a place where it is usual to see ibex. Eventually the path makes a big loop left then right to surmount a big hump. A level bottomed hollow is reached where *névé* is likely but the path quickly leaves on the right and makes a series of easy zigzags across screes. Towards the summit the path narrows and the footing becomes rather greasy and steep. The apparent top turns out to be false. A chain handrail starts here (of dubious utility) and takes you across the top of a scree filled gully to the true col. The path descends steeply on the other side and leads you down below the sombre wall of the Punta Bianca, in interminable zigzags, until you traverse left into a second valley, the Vallone dell'Inferno. There is a junction where the VA4 and VA2 part company.

The next part of this section includes a steep via ferrata. If you wish to avoid this then descend to Eaux Rousses on the VA2 path and walk up the road to Pont. If you are continuing on the VA4 then go left and walk up past the chalets of Levionaz d'en haut. The path climbs easy, grassy slopes to the top of an old, vegetated moraine which gives views of the glaciers of Gran Neyron and Timorion. Climb the bare moraine on the left using the yellow waymarks as a guide. Cross the river and continue to climb moraine on the other side with the ice of the glacier of Gran Neyron on your left. The goal is a small gap in the ridge ahead which is not easy to see from here but the cliff below is cut by a fissure which indicates the route you are to follow. Just below this point the route climbs past a patch of *névé* and a ladder can be seen climbing a small buttress. Cross towards this with the help of a fixed rope, over mixed scree and ice, and climb the ladder and the isolated rungs above to land on a wide shelf. Waist sling and karabiner will prove useful here and above. A long chain starts at the rear of the shelf. It is well anchored and allows you to climb the several tens of metres of exposed rock to arrive at the gap of the Col du Grand Neyron. Here there is a flat rock where you cross the ridge and have a view of the Montandayne glacier.

The terrain now becomes very broken and the waymarks are extremely useful. Descend almost directly, then go right traversing the slopes below the Punta Money. (A good mule track goes left, though where or why I cannot say. Presumably much has been destroyed by rockfalls and snow.) Scramble among the rocks, losing height slowly, then a little faster on a better path but still hugging the mountain wall. Eventually the path turns away from this and

The Gran Neyron glacier on the approach to the Col du Gran Neyron

traverses pleasant, easy ground making for the ridge called the Costa Savolera which hides the Rifugio Chabod from you until the last few minutes. It is possible to return to the valley from this point.

Third section: Rif. Chabod to Pont: 3h for 940m of descent and 150m ascent. From the refuge you go down to the river, the Torrente Costa Savolere, and cross this by a good bridge. This is much higher than the crossing marked on my IGC map and I suspect that the retreat of the glaciers has allowed the path to take a higher line than indicated. A good path takes you south towards the Rif. Vittorio Emanuele though it undulates considerably and is not as fast as might be though for an apparent traverse. One can visit the refuge or by-pass it and descend the zigzags directly to the valley. Pont is reached by following the river north to a bridge near the campsite.

Stage 3:
PONT TO RIFUGIO BENEVOLO IN VAL DI RHÊMES

Grade: 4 or strenuous 3 depending on route taken.

Time needed: 6h 40m. Height gain 1150m and descent 900m. Map IGC 102. The routes are all on Map 10 (p90).

Comment: A very scenic part of the route with blue lakes and glaciers. Can be broken at Rif. Savoia or Rif. Citta di Chivasso.

Route: The route has several variants, all of which are shown on the map. There are two possibilities from Pont into the Piano del Nivolet of which one, via the Grand Collet, will be described later as a day tour. The usual route, which has less ascent, starts behind the Hotel Paradis and climbs slightly among blocks and trees making for the steep cliff ahead. At the foot of this cliff the path starts to climb in earnest up a series of zigzags to bring you to a fine cross, the Croce Arolley, which marks the end of the hanging valley, the Piano del Nivolet, and is already some 300m above Pont. You pass smooth slabs and rocks and enter the rather dull levels of the valley where the beauty of the scenery around is hidden from you. Pass the

The Levanna from Alpi Rama on the way down from
Colle Sia to Ceresole Reale

Col de la Terra. Lago Lillet is the other side of the col. (GTGP)
From the west side of the Colle dei Becchi with the Levanna peaks in the distance and the Bochetta del Ges with mist behind. (GTGP)

Alp du Grand Collet and climb obliquely the valley side on the right making for the road which reaches here over the Col del Nivolet. This is very much a tourist area and people picnic in mass around the Lagi del Nivolet. The Rif. Savoia is opposite the first lake and the Rif. Citta di Chivasso is visible near the top of the Col del Nivolet. To see the view into the upper Valle di Locana it is necessary to walk a little south past this second refuge, to a belvedere on the road.

If using the Grand Collet route you should allow about 2 hours for the extra 400m ascent and descent.

The route continues from the Rif. Savoia by taking a path which climbs just behind the refuge, or from the Rif. Citta di Chivasso by dropping down the road a little to the north and taking a path which traverses gently from a little car park on the left. Both paths takes you onto a level area, the Piani del Rosset, which is studded with lakes and where the proximity of the road means that there are many paths. It will be seen on Map 10 that three routes exist to join the heads of these two valleys.

Variation 1: Col Rosset (3023m)
This is the standard VA4 route and is the one upon which the times and height gain is based. It is the most used of the three variations and is grade 3 but very steep on the western side of the col.

Climb behind the Rif. Savoia to the Alpage Riva and continue over less steep ground to the Piani del Rosset. Cross the outlet of Lac Rosset and follow a path which goes between this and Lac Leità. The path then climbs steeply and reaches an undulating scree with little lakes in the hollows. Make for the foot of the wall below Col Rosset and follow a well formed but steep zigzag path to the summit. There is plenty of room for lunch and it is also possible to follow the ridge on the right towards the Punta Leynir, which gives an excellent view of the col. To continue to the Benevolo refuge, go a little left as seen from the path used for the ascent, and find a path which descends over a cream coloured, sandy scree and then traverses left. After a short distance the rocks darken and you are committed to a steep and at times awkward descent over a surface varying from big blocks to fine scree and which drops over 400m in 1km. Eventually, the path reaches a group of very large boulders and the slope eases. Continue over pasture towards the Alpage la Grand Vaudelaz, near

Lagi di Trebecchi from Leynir path, Gran Paradiso behind

where the path forks. You take to the left a little before the chalets and cross the river on an adequate bridge. A large stone is painted with the name of your destination, in case you have doubts. The path now makes a mostly gentle climbing traverse onto the shoulder of the hillside on the left, contours round this and then makes a gradual descent over rather wet ground where the line of the path is occasionally doubtful, to reach the track up the Val di Rhêmes a little below the refuge.

It is possible to continue to Thumel from the Grand Vaudelaz by following the path which keeps the river on the left, though this involves unnecessary loss of height when making for the Benevolo and is really only useful if you wish to go to Rhêmes Notre Dame.

Variation 2: Colle del Nivoletta (3130m)
This is, strictly speaking, part of the GTGP but is a much more splendid route and some parties may prefer to use it in preference to Col Rosset. It is more difficult at grade 4 and involves slightly more climbing. The path used for the ascent from the Nivolet is quite busy and well marked and appears to be a standard way to visit the Punta Basei, most walkers returning to the Col del Nivolet.

Gran Paradiso from above Nivolet

The path on to the Benevolo is less evident and some routefinding skill is required but the views of the glaciers and peaks along the Franco-Italian frontier are absolutely magnificent. In places one is looking directly into crevasses across the valley.

Route: If starting at the Rif. Chivasso, walk down the road to a sharp bend where there is some off-road parking on the left. If starting at the Rif. Savoia, walk up to the same place.

A path strikes off north-west and soon has a stream on the left which it crosses below a waterfall. It now climbs more steeply to a level area, passes a small lake and then goes past the southern end of Lago Leità. Climb again to a path junction where go right and climb to a rocky bulge at the end of a line of cliffs. Either climb easy rocks on the left or follow the line of a little chimney on the right. This section poses the only technical difficulties of the whole walk. You arrive on a broad, grassy terrace with a good path. This is followed onto scree above the cliffs. The angle is easy and the scree ledge is wide so that there is remarkably little sense of exposure, considering the position of the path. *Névé* alternates with rock and scree and eventually leads to the Col Basei.

Lago Leità, from Nivoletta path

The view from this high path is of exceptional beauty. The mountain scenery is grand and is enhanced by the presence of some thirteen natural lakes of all sizes niched blue in folds of the hills. Underfoot is also made attractive by the presence of abundant *Campanula cenisia* and *Saxifraga biflora* with occasional *Linaria alpina* and *Geum reptans*.

The Punta Basei lies to the left and is worth a visit. The ridge leading to it is followed initially without any real difficulty, taking you alongside the bergschrund of the Basei glacier. A more difficult slabby section follows and then the ridge is crossed to its left to bring you to a corner just below the summit. There is a window in the rock which gives airy views to the west, and a small shrine. The last few metres to the summit is a short rock climb which is exposed over a 500m drop into the Vallone della Gavite and so should not be attempted without a rope. I am told that there was a cable installed here to allow safe access to the summit but heavy winter's snow has carried this away. Return to Col Basei using the ascent route.

In order to continue towards the Refuge Benevolo, walk down the ridge (ie. go right from the ascent path) towards the Colle del

Nivoletta. In fact one never actually gets there, despite the maps, but after walking across a broad, stony ridge you will come to a pile of greenish rocks with a boulder field beyond leading to the col. Turn left here and quickly find a faint but definite path which plunges down a scree hillside. The route is marked by cairns. The path goes right at first, following a scree rib then traverses left to avoid cliffs and eventually brings you to the summit of a moraine. This is followed for a while but do not go too far as it ends in steep cliffs. Look for a big cairn, then for some rounded, reddish rocks below on the left and make for these down the side of the moraine. This brings you into a broad valley which leads down without incident. The cairns are not much help here but reappear in sparse but sufficient quantity to conduct you down towards an area of whitish stones where you pass below an enormous boulder, then follow gravel stream beds to emerge on grassy pastures. The path now runs parallel to the river and above an impressive gorge to arrive at the refuge without further incident.

Somewhat disconcertingly, on the last part of this stage and near the Benevolo, a large stone will be seen up on the right which bears the legend "Colle di Nivoletta" and an arrow pointing back, so suggesting that you are off route. The guardienne at the refuge, however, informed me that this is a path which takes you to the shapely, pyramidal peak north of the col.

Variation 3: Col Leynir (3084m)
This is not strictly part of either the GTGP or the VA4 but will be included here since there is a report implying that it can be used as such. The climb to the Col Leynir from the Col del Nivolet is grade 4 but if you make the full crossing to Thumel it is 4M.

Time needed: 2h to the col, 2$^{1}/_{2}$h minimum for the descent to Val di Rhêmes. The descent to Thumel is 1200m.

Comment: The ascent from the Col del Nivolet is pleasant, passing several lakes, and takes you eventually into an ochre alpine desert. You are almost certain to encounter patches of *névé*, some steep, and a ski pole is almost essential. If making the full crossing to Val di Rhêmes, the descent from the col follows the edge of the small Glacier di Vaudalettaz and an

Lac Rosset with Punta Basei and Colle del Nivoletta behind

ice axe is essential. It has been suggested that this crossing may be part of the VA4. It is not in fact so waymarked and the upper part of the path down to Val di Rhêmes is almost non-existent. Nor is it as direct a crossing to the Benevolo hut as is Col Rosset but involves a climb back up the valley once Thumel has been reached. For most fell walkers I suspect that it should be regarded as a place for a return visit from the Col del Nivolet. A well worthwhile trip, nevertheless.

Ascent: Take a path which starts at a small car park just below the Rifugio Citta di Chivasso and follow this to a junction with a path below a little cascade. This new path starts at the Rifugio Savoia and this is an alternative start. Follow this path, keeping the cascade on your left, to a flattish area called the Piani del Rosset. The path climbs steadily above Lac Rosset which is below you on your left. You are led steadily upward into more and more austere terrain. The Lagi di Trebecchi come into view for a while and then you climb into a small valley which takes you over a small col to the Vallone Leynir, with signs of a made up mule track. Descend into the valley and follow a series of climbing traverses to reach the col. A path goes off on the right to a small shoulder which is a good viewpoint. Return to the Col del Nivolet by the same route.

Descent to Val di Rhêmes: Step onto the glacier just below the col and follow this down on *névé*, keeping to the right. The map shows you descending on scree but this looks awkward and would only be necessary if the glacier were clear of *névé* and smooth, clear ice predominated. There are one or two outcrops of stone below so do not get out of control! Once onto the moraine, the map is misleading as the route it suggests does not look very practicable. Follow the centre of the moraine in a direction a little north of north-west and manoeuvring so that you are always descending ground that is visible ahead. The stream issuing from the moraine is not marked on the map but keep a little right of this, and one or two footprints might be found. Descend on turf heading for the path, now visible below, in the Vallone della Vaudalettaz, and follow this down to the alp of the same name, whence a path takes you down steadily, then steeply through the forest to Thumel.

Stage 4:
RIFUGIO BENEVOLO TO RIFUGIO BEZZI IN VALGRISENCHE

Grade: 4

Time needed: 4h 40m. Height gain and descent 800m. Map IGC No.102. See Map 11 (p104).

Comment: Another day close to the glaciers.

Route: Go west behind the refuge and follow a path to a small arch bridge over the river and descend a little before starting to climb past an isolated building and soon start traversing left. This is not the red line marked on my map as Δ4 but joins the path marked in black. It is, however, satisfactorily waymarked. After a while you reach a flat stone on which directions have been painted: you need to go slightly right and upwards. The path now climbs quite steeply

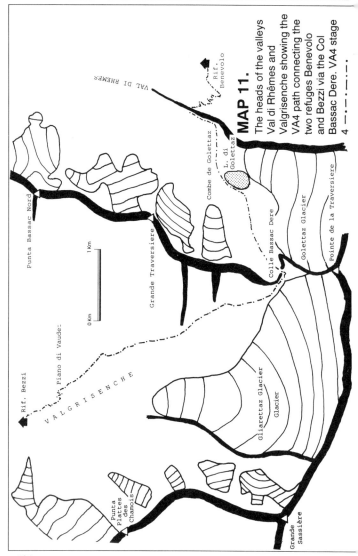

VAL DI RHÊMES

Rif. Benevolo

MAP 11.

The heads of the valleys
Val di Rhêmes and
Valgrisenche showing the
VA4 path connecting the
two refuges Benevolo
and Bezzi via the Col
Bassac Dere. VA4 stage
4 –·–·–·–·–·

L. di
Golettaz

Combe de Golettaz

Colle Bassac Dere

Golettaz Glacier

Pointe de la Traversière

Grande Traversière

Punta Bassac Nord

1 Km

0 Km

Piano di Vaudez

VALGRISENCHE

Rif. Bezzi

Gliarettaz Glacier

Glacier

Punta Plattes
des
Chamois

Grande
Sassière

through rocky bluffs and brings you onto the ridge separating the Val di Rhêmes from the Combe de Golettaz. A small lake is visible below. Follow this ridge up, passing from one side to another until you can cross to a flat moraine plain at about 2750m altitude. Cross this towards the Lago di Golettaz. This glacier lake at the foot of the Golettaz glacier is very impressive with the steep glacier snout plunging into the water. The lake is not marked on the IGC maps, presumably because the ice has retreated since the ground was surveyed. Cross the stream near where it emerges from the lake and then walk across morain, tending right with cairns and waymarks to guide you. The Colle Bassac Dere is visible as the lowest gap ahead (3082m) and to the right of the glacier. The path climbs steadily through scree to the col and makes a final short, but very steep, climb to the crest. Here you are looking straight into the crevasses of the Gliarettaz glacier with the Italian wall of the Aiguille de la Grande Sassière behind. Descend the other side of the col, which is again steep, and as the slope eases follow the path to the right, so keeping away from the glacier and traversing below the rocks of the Punta Bassac Dere. The glacier marked here on the map is no longer there. The path loses very little height; indeed sections of ascent are encountered. Eventually, as the moorland of the Piano di Vaudet comes into view, the path turns down and zigzags to a lower level whence it makes a generally descending traverse, at one point through some enormous blocks of rock, to the Bezzi hut. The route is well waymarked, which is as well, because it does not seem to correspond completely with any of the paths marked on my IGC map.

Stage 5:
RIFUGIO BEZZI IN VALGRISENCHE TO LA THUILE

Grade:	3 with a short section of 4.
Time needed:	14$^{1}/_{2}$h. Height gain 1964m and descent 2800m. Maps IGC Nos.102 & 107, IGN No.3532ET in TOP25 series. Route is on Map 12 (p106).
Comment:	This stage covers much the same ground as stage 2 of the VA2 and little extra description is needed.

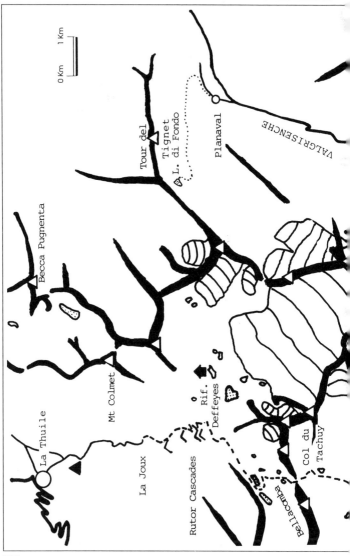

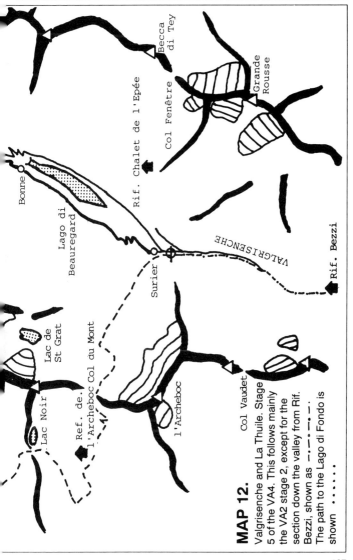

MAP 12.

Valgrisenche and La Thuile. Stage 5 of the VA4. This follows mainly the VA2 stage 2, except for the section down the valley from Rif. Bezzi, shown as –·–·–·– . The path to the Lago di Fondo is shown · · · · · ·

On the map of Valgrisenche the VA4 is shown as climbing to Lago St Grat then to the Scavarda Refuge whence it descends to Planaval and follows the crossing via the Col de Planaval which has already been discussed. The Scavarda Refuge was burned down some years ago and a woman lost her life in the fire. The refuge has essentially been abandoned, perhaps as a sad memorial to this tragedy. I have not followed this route.

Route: Go north from the Bezzi hut on a path which descends steeply and is awkward in places. The track marked as going to the hut on my IGC map is a delusion though it appears lower down the valley and makes for easy progress to Surier. This is reached by taking the first left turn over the river where you are now on a road. A little way up the road, just before the next bridge (spectacular at that!), there is a path marked as going off left and which leads along the valley bottom to the Col du Mont. One can, however, gain height more easily by following the road until a track is reached which goes off left to Grand Alpage. When I first did this it was possible to use a path which cut the bends of the road but the road has since been much improved and I do not think that this is now practicable. After this, one is simply reversing the VA2 route already described. The most demanding part is the Col du Tachuy but as the stage has to be broken at one of two French refuges prior to this climb, you can fortify yourself with French food and wine, so also having a change from the Italian fare.

Stage 6:
LA THUILE TO COURMAYEUR

Grade: Mostly 2 or 3 but cut by two points of great difficulty between the Colle di Bassa Serra and the Colle di Chavannes which are 4M.

Time needed: 10h. Height gain 1340m, descent 1580m. The stage can be broken at the Elizabetta Refuge. Map IGC No.107. The route is on Map 13 (p110).

Comment: This is the second difficult stage of the VA4. There are two difficult sections, neither of which is protected. The first to be encountered is the descent from the Colle di Bassa Serra. This is a descending traverse on narrow ledges across a small rock face with steep scree below and is thus quite exposed though the footing is good. The second is the crossing of the couloir of Mt Lechaud. The face of this mountain, which has an average angle of 38°, is cleft by a shallow couloir which is crossed by the path. This is raked by avalanches in winter so that it has proved impossible to keep a chain in place. In spring the couloir is full of hard snow and cannot be crossed safely, without the proper mountaineering equipment, until the snow has gone, or almost so. It can thus only be crossed by a walking party later in the season. It is a delicate passage and needs care. These two difficult passages can only be avoided by using the path up the Vallone di Chavannes, that is, the VA2 route.

Route: Leave La Thuile by the road taking the direction of the Col du Petit St Bernard. One or two short cuts are possible on waymarked paths (O10) but you are making for the hairpin bend near La Cretaz at about 1850m. A track goes off the outside of the bend and is signposted to the Bassa Serra. The track drops a little and you will see a bridge on the right which crosses the river. Descend to this using either of the evident paths and continue left up the valley on a path. This eventually reaches a track, cuts across it and meets it again a little higher. Follow the track left to a wide turning area above Plan Veyle. A path climbs back on the right and this soon reaches a fork where you go left and follow a path which makes an undulating traverse of the side of the Vallone del Breuil. Note that the paths shown on my IGC map are not laid out as described above. Climb gently to Entre Deux Eaux where there are some ruined buildings a little off the path and climb quite steeply to pass a little reservoir. All along this section you are opposite an impressive rock wall on the other side of the valley down which water cascades. The

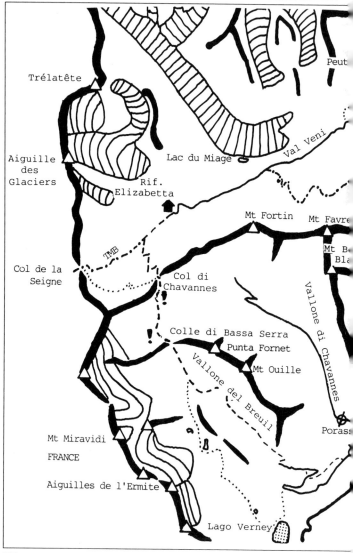

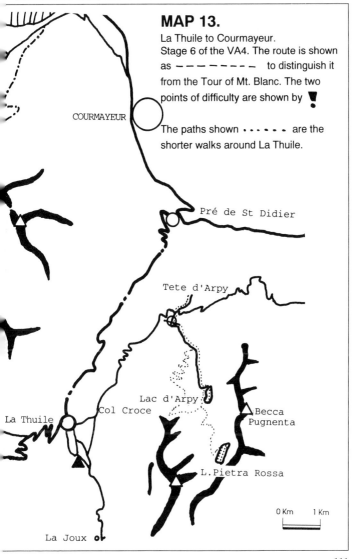

MAP 13.

La Thuile to Courmayeur.
Stage 6 of the VA4. The route is shown
as – – – – – – – – to distinguish it
from the Tour of Mt. Blanc. The two
points of difficulty are shown by ❗

The paths shown • • • • • are the
shorter walks around La Thuile.

COURMAYEUR

Pré de St Didier

Tete d'Arpy

Lac d'Arpy

Col Croce

Becca
Pugnenta

La Thuile

L.Pietra Rossa

0 Km   1 Km

La Joux

The Aiguille des Glaciers and the Trélatête from the Colle di Bassa Serra.
The couloir of Mt Lechaud is in the foreground with the
Colle di Chavannes to its left

path now makes a more gentle climbing traverse left over the steep ground which forms the apparent head of the valley, to reach a little col at about 2580m. There is a cairn on a hump to the left of the col. At this point you realise that you have not climbed out of the valley but have, rather, climbed into its upper part. Descend to a level area and then follow the path ahead which climbs gently but steadily to the Colle di Bassa Serra where you arrive beside a ruined building with the message "Fine Sentiero" painted on its wall. I suppose that this is to discourage walkers from attempting the next section. This is a superb spot with a desert moraine field below, Mt Lechaud and the Colle di Chavannes visible ahead, all with a backdrop of Mt Blanc.

To continue, go left past the ruin and walk along the broad ridge of the col to a large cairn and a rock waymarked Δ4. A path descends on your right towards the moraine field and quickly ends in a little hollow. From this point you have to traverse on little ledges until you can step down onto scree. Continue a little way then go back

The Mt Lechaud couloir and the morain desert below the Colle di Bassa Serra. The path can just be made out where it crosses the wall of the couloir

113

right near the foot of the cliff you have just crossed until you can go more or less straight down.

Note that if coming in the opposite direction, this traverse is difficult to see as the rocks face north and the light is in your eyes. To locate the path look at the rocks below the big cairn on the ridge. A yellow band of rock will be seen which is wide at the left, under the cairn, but narrows to almost nothing to the right. The first few steps of the path use ledges in the narrow part of the yellow band.

To continue, when you reach level ground, you will see that the Chavannes glacier is only a shadow of its former self as marked on the maps and that the ice is miles away above you. Descend a little way to a black boulder streaked with white. At this point it should be possible to see a cairn on the left. Go towards this to find a path which takes you through the wilderness. Someone has, in the past, cleared large stones from this path and placed them in two parallel lines on either side to mark the way and there are also cairns. (These parallel lines of stones also mark the path on the way up to the Bassa Serra.) The path takes a line generally north-west passing several little lakes and eventually crossing stepping stones over a shallow stream to a path which runs parallel with the stream. Go right, towards the Mt Lechaud couloir.

The path rounds a little ridge and arrives on a ledge which cuts the steep, near wall of the couloir. The place is quite exposed but the ledge is wide. You descend from the end of the ledge into the couloir on fine black scree with ample hand holds. When I did this there was a slab of snow ice in the bed of the gully and it was necessary to descend slightly to pass below this and traverse to the other wall of the couloir. This is where, if the couloir were full of ice, it would be necessary to retreat. The opposite side is effectively a great slab but covered with little ledges (and loose stones). You cross to the rock and land on quite small holds then traverse on ledges which steadily increase in breadth and open out into a path which takes you directly to the Colle di Chavannes, another splendid viewpoint.

The way to Courmayeur is now evident and is the reversal of the route described for the first stage of the VA2.

The Grand Traverse of the Gran Paradiso: the GTGP

One end of this walk starts in Valgrisenche and follows the line of the VA4 as far as the Col del Nivolet, using the variation via the Colle del Nivoletta. From the Col del Nivolet, it traverses east to follow the line of the Orco valley, but high up on the south facing slopes, and in doing so it enters much wilder country. Chamois and ibex are encountered everywhere and most of the time you will be very much on your own. I have the impression that the eastern part of this route is little used. The paths deteriorate as one moves from west to east and, past the Rif. Pocchiolo Meneghello, there is a glacier crossing to be made which, while classed as easy, is possibly best avoided by the average British fellwalker. In addition, the accommodation on this route is rather meagre and depends on bivouacs, of which only one, the Ivrea, is of any size with 9 beds. There is one guarded refuge, the Pontese, and one unguarded, the Pocchiolo Meneghello, but these are close together and do not provide alternatives to the bivouacs. The walk ends "officially" at Campiglia Soana but I have decided to describe it only as far as the Rif. Meneghello. The descent to the valley from this refuge is long and does not have the best of paths and while it is of interest, some may prefer to return over the Bocchetta di Valsoera and make the much easier descent on the track below the dam of the Lago di Telecchio.

The waymarking in this part of the park is less ostentatious than in the Valdotain and consists mostly of slashes of dull red paint, not always easy to follow in a mist.

A glossary is not needed for this walk as the maps are all agreed on the nomenclature, presumably as we are more deeply into Italy.

The first two stages have already been described as parts of the VA4 and will only be described briefly below, in the reverse direction.

Finally, it should also be remarked that the weather here seems less reliable than in the rest of the Gran Paradiso, an observation

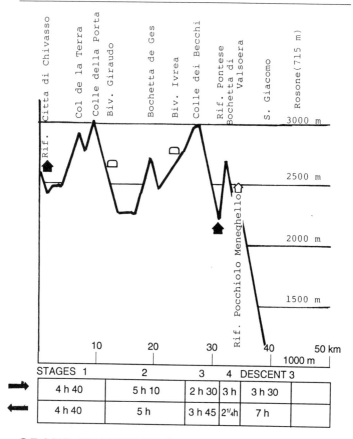

GRAND TRAVERSE OF THE GRAN PARADISO HEIGHT & DISTANCE CHART (Stage 3 only)

Only the third stage is shown as the first and second are identical to the Via Alta 4. Standard times are given for each section, for either direction of walking. Refuges are shown 🛑 , unguarded refuges ⬆ and bivouacs ◻.

based on four visits when my activities were terminated by the arrival of bad weather although it remained fine further west.

The total distance for the route described is 73km and the total ascent is 4610m and descent around 5590m, depending on the route chosen to descend to the valley.

Stage 1:
VALGRISENCHE TO RIFUGIO BENEVOLO

Grade:	4.
Comment:	The route described in Berutto's guide climbs from Planaval to the Rif. Scavarda which has been destroyed by fire. It then descends to Surier and so to the Rif. Bezzi. This involves almost 12 hours' walking without intermediate accommodation and so is perhaps impracticable. I suggest two alternatives: either on the opposite side of the valley, via the Chalet de l'Epée, or along the valley bottom if time is short, though this involves a lot of walking on the road. The stage can be broken either at Rif. Bezzi or the Epée.
Time needed:	Via the Epée, 10h 20m with 1900m of ascent and 1270m of descent.
Via the valley,	7h 50m for 1430m of ascent and 800m of descent. The last, common section between the Rifs. Bezzi and Benevolo takes 4h 50m. Map IGC No.102. Maps 6 (p66) and 12 (p106).
Approach:	It is assumed that you will start in Valgrisenche village.

Route:
Via the Chalet de l'Epée. Follow the VA2 by Benevy and Le Bois as described in detail for stage 2 of the VA2. From the Chalet, descend to the Alp de l'Epée and follow the path to the Alp du Mont Forclaz and down through the old larch forest to the track, where you go left and continue down to the junction with the track in the bottom of the valley. Go left to climb, gently at first, to the Rif. Bezzi.

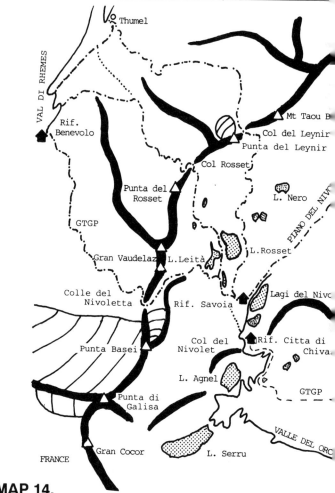

MAP 14.

The region around the Colle de Nivolet showing the line of the VA4 —•—•—
and the GTGP ———— . Stage 2 of the GTGP is shown and the first part of
stage 3 as far as the Bivouac Giraudo. Path •••• is the Gran Collet route.

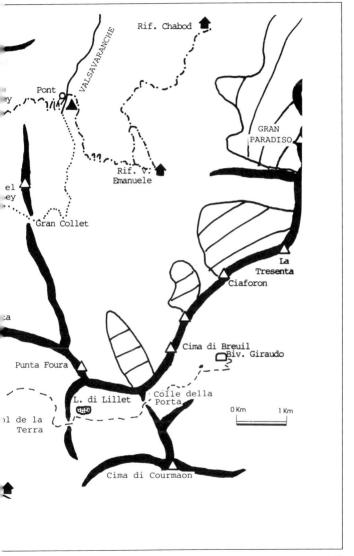

Via the valley bottom. Take the road to the Beauregard dam and then along the eastern side of the lake on a narrow, twisting road to the junction just past Uselères. The road then becomes a track which takes you towards Rif. Bezzi, the last part being a steep climb on a path.

Rif. Bezzi to Rif. Benevolo. This is the reverse of stage 4 of the Via Alta 4. Follow the path south from Rif. Bezzi which climbs steadily and passes among some big blocks. A little later it climbs more steeply and then follows an undulating traverse to the Colle Bassac Dere. The last few metres of ascent to the col are steep, as is the short descent on the other side. The path then leads steadily down to the glacier lake, which is not shown on the IGC maps. Pass round this on its left, cross the outlet and make for the ridge which separates the Combe de Golettaz from Rif. Benevolo. The ridge is followed down past the point 2735m to above a little lake where a path takes you right and down towards the refuge. On my IGC map are marked a steep ascent above Rif. Bezzi at the start and a path which keeps to the left of the Golettaz Combe: neither of these seem now to be used.

Stage 2:
RIFUGIO BENEVOLO TO THE COL DEL NIVOLET

Grade:	4.
Time needed:	4$^{1/}$2h. Ascent 845m and descent 524m. Map IGC No.102. Map 14 (p118).
Comment:	A magnificent day's walking.

Route: This is variation 2 of stage 3 of the VA4 but in reverse. Follow the river which passes behind the refuge, in a south-east direction, keeping the river on your right. The approximate line is marked 13b on my IGC map. You come to gravel stream beds and make for some whitish rocks where you pass beneath an enormous boulder. There is a large glacier moraine ridge on the left of the valley ahead. Make for the broad moraine valley below and to the right of this and gain height until it is possible to climb onto the crest of the moraine on your left. There are cairns on the crest which can be followed right to the Colle del Nivoletta. You in fact arrive on a ridge at a pile of greenish rocks with the real col on the left. Go right and climb to a point where it is possible to descend easily to the *névé* and go down left to the Col del Nivolet. This part of the route is normally well trodden. The only remaining difficulty is the descent off the end of the terrace just above Lago Leità.

Stage 3:
COL DEL NIVOLET TO RIFUGIO POCCHIOLO MENEGHELLO

Comment:	This stage comprises the whole of the remainder of the route that I shall describe. It will be divided into sections. It never descends below 2200m and there is little accommodation. It is therefore necessary to carry food, a small stove and a torch. Blankets are provided in the various shelters and a sheet sleeping bag is all that is necessary in the way of bedding.

Section 1. Col del Nivolet to Bivouac Margherita Giraudo

Grade:	Initially 2 then 3 with some 4.
Time needed:	4h 40m for 730m of ascent and 630m of descent. Map IGC No.102 and passing onto No.101. Map 14 (P118).
Comment:	A crossing of two high cols which takes you below the rock walls which form the southern side of the big, glaciated summits which surround the head of Valsavaranche. The Bivouac Giraudo has six beds. Unfortunately, in season, it is likely to be crowded as people seem to come up from Ceresole Reale to spend the night. There were ten of us when I spent the night there, and it is probably preferable to continue to the Bivouac Ivrea which is bigger and more isolated. There are several escape routes to the Orco valley: to Alpi Chiapili (signpost), to Ceresole from Lago Lillet, and to Ceresole from

Biv. Giraudo. This last is the only one I have done and the section Col del Nivolet - Biv. Giraudo - Ceresole is an excellent walk in its own right which could be used as a fitting end to the walk if time was limited or the weather turned sour.

Route: From the Col del Nivolet follow the road in the direction of Lago Agnel or use the mule track which starts at the Rif. Citta di Chivasso and takes the more direct line. At an altitude of 2461m there is a flattish area with a little lake to the east, and a rather obtrusive power line. A good path starts here and passes round the lake, climbs a little and then traverses east. After about 2$^{1}/_{2}$km the path starts to climb again as you make for the col de la Terra. A climbing traverse is made to below the col then a final traverse on the slopes of the Punta Rochetta. The col is spacious and covered with fine scree which perhaps gives it its name. The next objective, the Colle della Porta, can be seen, but not Lago Lillet.

Descend from the col to the lake on a mule track which descends steep ground and is much deteriorated in places. The lake soon comes into view and the path crosses its outlet. There is a path which goes right, to Ceresole, just after this point. Continue in an easterly direction, climbing on moraine and making for the right-hand side of the Colle della Porta. The Glacier Della Porta is much smaller than indicated on the map but it is necessary for the last 200m or so to traverse across this to gain the col. If the ice is covered with snow there is no real problem though were the ice bare it would be necessary to take to the scree just above the edge of the glacier. The col is again quite spacious.

To continue, follow the mule track which descends below you in zigzags and then climbs a little again to the right to avoid some awkward country. Again, the track is deteriorated in places, but still makes good footing even if you have to be careful where you tread. Eventually, you reach a little level spot with a stream running through, though this is not marked on the map. The altitude is about 2600m. By now we have left the tourist hordes behind and you will be unlucky not to start seeing ibex or chamois, or both.

If you are making for the Biv. Giraudo, go left of a little knoll marked as 2679m on the map and descend a stony gully to another

Descending from the Col de la Terra to Lago Lillet. The path round the outlet is visible and is typical of a well preserved mule track

flattish area by a bigger stream which is in the upper part of the Vallone del Roc. Across the stream there is a little passage behind a knoll. Cross the steam and pass behind the knoll to meet up with the path which climbs to the bivouac. This is never visible to you, but if you now climb the path you encounter first a large cairn and the shelter is just a little way behind. Water is available in the little Lago Piatta. This section between the two paths is not waymarked.

If you are not visiting the Biv. Giraudo, you may still wish to go this way for the sake of seeing the fauna. Or, as you arrive at the first flat place before the gully, you will see a big cairn on the right which, I believe, signals the mule track which descends directly to Alpi di Breuil and so misses out the stony gully. I was in mist at this point and could not be sure but I have subsequently seen from afar that there is indeed a track or path here. This path takes you down to a large plain area criss-crossed by rivers and with a lake and which we cross in the early part of the next section.

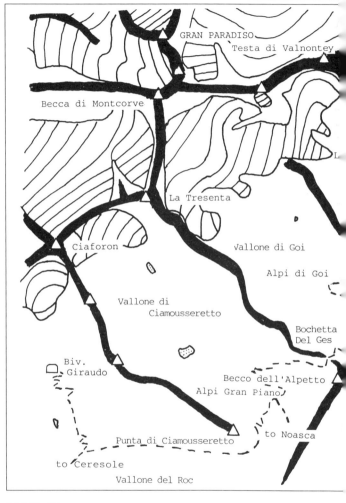

MAP 15.

Vallone del Roc, Vallone di Noaschetta and Vallone di Piantonetto, showing the line of the GTGP from Bivouac Giraudo to Rifugio Pontese.

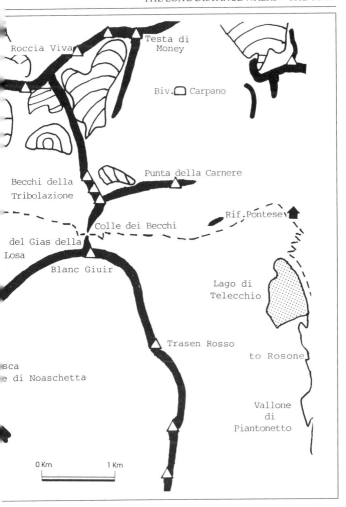

The starts of four routes to the valley, to Ceresole, to Noasca and to Rosone are shown.

125

Section 2. Bivouac Giraudo to Bivouac Ivrea

Grade: 3, then 4 over the Bochetta del Ges, then 2 to the Ivrea.

Time needed: 5h 10m for a total ascent of 700m and a descent of 570m. Map IGC No.101. Map 15 (p124).

Comment: A descent followed by a traverse into the Vallone di Ciamousseretto which is quitted by the Bochetta del Ges to arrive in the Vallone di Noaschetta at a place isolated and deep in the hills. An easy walk follows up the tributary valley, the Vallone del Gias della Losa, through magnificent rock scenery. The Ivrea has 9 beds and is more spacious than the Giraudo. It is also more isolated and, I suspect, less likely to be crowded than the Giraudo.

Route: From the Bivouac Giraudo follow a good path down through rocky terrain to arrive at a large, flat area which is an alluvial plain, with a small lake. Such flat, alluvial areas are a feature of this part of the Gran Paradiso and we will cross several in our travels. The path from the Bivouac Giraudo follows the eastern edge of the plain then descends quite steeply again to reach a path junction where a rock is painted with the direction "Alpi Gran Piano" for the branch going east. The path going west takes you to Ceresole Reale and is one escape route but also a fine walk in itself which we will describe shortly. The path east makes a slightly rising traverse of the slopes of the Cresta di Ciamousseretto on a fold in the ground which was probably a mule track at one time but is now a ledge with a path running along the centre. Eventually, you round the end of the Ciamousseretto ridge and descend on a good track to pass below some cliffs with the national park building visible on the Alpi Gran Piano ahead. It is possible to get to the Alp by crossing a bridge or by following the path around with the stream on the right. A group was picnicking near the building, with a rather strangely dressed walker standing just above them. As I got nearer I realised that this was a life-sized statue of the Virgin. It is possible to cross the alluvial flat to the building, where there is water on tap, but our path continues on a mule track which climbs the hillside behind and is making for the Vallone di Ciamousseretto.

Bivouac Ivrea with the Testa di Tribolazione and Testa di Valnontey behind

Follow this track, which is in quite good condition, as far as a rounded, rocky knoll marked on the map as 2434m. There is a junction here and you take the right-hand fork, now making for the Bochetta del Ges. The track is reasonable at first but as you climb below the cliffs ahead, it virtually disappears from time to time, destroyed by rock falls. There are three places of this sort and in each case it seems best to scramble up, tending right a little to rediscover the track. Near the col a virtual motorway of a track is followed but this deteriorates below the final climb to the col and it is again necessary to pick your way to the top.

The top is spacious with good views. A good track descends into the Vallone di Noaschetta and then makes a horizontal traverse right. It becomes much deteriorated but not difficult. The ground below is much more broken and rocky than the map suggests and there is no point in trying to descend directly. The path takes you round into a broad gully with a col at its summit which is the Bochetta dell' Alpetto. This is given as an alternative route by Berutto, linking Gran Piano with Vallone di Noaschetta. It is said to be waymarked, though the route described is not. Descend the gully. There is a mule track but this has been almost entirely obliterated by a thin layer of sliding scree and the surface is quite treacherous. The path eventually improves and takes you quickly down to join the path from Noasca to the Bivouac Ivrea. The mule track from this point is excellent and takes you left, down to the river, and then follows this past Alpi la Bruna and up into the Vallone di Goi. Here the path makes an ample right-hand bend past another alluvial flat to reverse direction and make for the Alpi la Motta. A rusty signpost shows where to turn off. You now enter the Vallone del Gias della Losa and have a magnificent view of the three pinnacles of the Becchi della Tribolazione and of the Colle dei Becchi, which is tomorrow's objective. The path leads to another alluvial plain and swings round to the left, with the bivouac in view, to turn due north across the flat at a point suggested by another rusty signpost. The map shows the path as passing to the right of the river and swinging back to the bivouac, and this might be preferable if there is a lot of water about. The bivouac stands on a knoll above the level of the plain with water about 20m away.

Lac d'Arpy, Grandes Jorasses behind. (SW)
Mt Blanc from Lago di Pietra Rossa. (SW)

Section 3. Bivouac Ivrea to Rifugio Pontese

Grade: 4 over the Colle dei Becchi, otherwise 3.

Time needed: This calculates to be $2^{1/2}$h but the going over the col is awkward and it can take appreciably longer than this. Map 15 (p124).

Comment: There are no waymarks between the bivouac and the col, nor any real path except at the start. Once over the col the way is well indicated - necessarily so, since this is a standard day outing from the Rif. Pontese. The cirque surrounding the Bivouac Ivrea is magnificent. I cannot comment on that around the Pontese as it has always been immersed in mist when I have been there. The Pontese is a large refuge with guardian, but it closes relatively early, though there is winter accommodation then left open. The name originates from the fact that the refuge was constructed at the behest of the alpinists of Pont Canavese. The refuge is easy of access since it is possible to drive up to the dam of the Lago di Telecchio.

Route: Looking east from the Bivouac Ivrea, a mule track can be seen climbing the hillside on the other side of the stream. Descend to the alluvial flat, cross the stream and join this track. It climbs gently and then turns the end of a low ridge where it goes north for a little, then makes a climbing traverse below the Becca della Losa. From the end of this ridge you look across a flat river bed which leads directly to the foot of the Colle dei Becchi. The way to the west side of the col is blocked by a big moraine heap except that on its left, where it touches the wall of the mountain above, there is a triangle of *névé*. Make directly for this, leaving the mule track, to follow the gravel river bed as convenient. Berutto suggests that one should follow the mule track until it is convenient to cross to a moraine of big blocks below the Becchi della Tribolazione which is crossed to the *névé* cone. This gains some height but crossing the moraine is slow going, even with one or two cairns to guide you. Climb the *névé* cone and eventually make for the blocks on its right side at whatever

Largo di Fondo with Rutor group behind

point you feel is convenient. Continue to climb, tending slightly right until a cairn is reached which signals the point at which you should start to make for the centre of the morain. The ground is now less steep and progress is aided by some patches of *névé*. Make for the right-hand side of the col and at its summit find a perch on the big blocks where a pause can be made. Note that there are equally big holes between the big blocks and some degree of care is needed in crossing this terrain.

To descend to the east, go to the edge of the blocks and take to the *névé*. There is an extensive slope which is quite steep in its centre, and ski pole or ice axe are almost essential. At the foot of the *névé* you enter a level hollow which is crossed to find cairn and waymarks. These take you easily over the top of the eastern moraine to its edge where a descent is made, tending left, over a mixture of fine scree and rock. This brings you to more level ground with some brownish rocks. Follow the waymarks and cairns with care here. They conduct you along a series of broad ledges which intersect rocky bluffs and cliffs to arrive in the bottom of the gully below the morain. The stream bed is followed as it is mostly dry, to pass through a sort of gate where the gully widens. The waymarks take you easily through more big scree to a little green oasis which is a pleasant place to stop. The cairns continue from here but there are no more waymarks for a while. Cross the green level to find a well defined path which takes you down to the refuge. This makes for the right of a rocky peak marked 2424m on the map and below which there are some ruined chalets. The Alpi Giafor is below you. You continue down to the river where some yellow waymarks direct you to a bridge across the stream. Follow the marks that keep to the top of the ridge. A short climb takes you to a good path on the other side of the river and you turn right for the Rifugio Pontese.

Note: A path is shown on the newer maps going left of point 2424, down a little valley, but this is not the best way.

Section 4. Rifugio Pontese to Rifugio Pocchiolo Meneghello

Grade: 4.

Time needed: 3h probably. I did this section in mist and there is a lot of traversing which is difficult to quantify from the map. Map 16 .

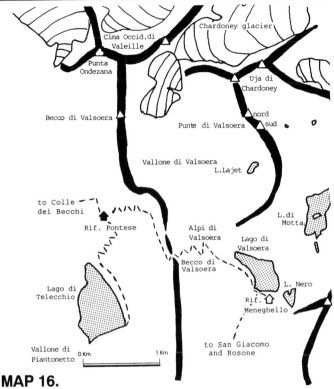

MAP 16.

Vallone di Piantonetto and Vallone di Valsoera, showing the line of the GTGP between Rifugio Pontese and Rifugio Pocchiola Meneghello and the start of the descent to the valley.

Comment: This is a very short section which would probably normally be combined with the previous one by most parties. The path is well waymarked and appears to cross some airy positions. The cirque of the Valsoera valley is wild and magnificent. Lago di Valsoera is an artificial lake and provides electricity for Turin. The Rifugio Pocchiolo Meneghello is a small wooden

131

cabin on stilts built just above the dam of the lake and has two rooms, the upper a dormitory with 14 beds. There is gas and a nearby water supply.

Route: The path is shown on my IGC map as starting at Muanda. In fact it starts from near the Rif. Pontese, which is situated on a shoulder immediately above the Lago di Telecchio. The path makes for a grassy rib east of the refuge and climbs this in tight zigzags. A short traverse around the head of a gully is exposed but otherwise the path is good.

Eventually, you climb to a sort of false col at about 2500m. The path now makes an undulating traverse right and crosses several ribs over more false cols until you reach a shallow gully which evidently will allow you to climb to the ridge and to the col, the Bocchetta di Valsoera. The path keeps out of the bed of the gully and follows grassy ledges among the rocks on the right to arrive at the spacious col. Two ways down are now possible: a high altitude route, which I did not do in view of the prevailing misty conditions, and the "easy" route which I followed. This descends the broad gully to the east of the Bocchetta di Valsoera, according to the map, making for the head of the Lago di Valsoera. This is a feasible route but there is a better alternative which is also waymarked. At about 2450m altitude there is a grassy ridge, covered with big rocks, which makes a descending traverse on your right. The crest of this is followed until you are above the lake. The lake in fact blocks the valley here and you have to traverse above it along a series of ledges with some necessary scrambling. The last few metres are across a little slab which has been provided with a chain handrail to assist your progress. You now cross the dam and go left to the refuge which is reached up what might have been an old inclined railway.

DESCENT ROUTES TO THE VALLEY

There are at least five along the route described and I have used three of them. Evidently, this stage can be shortened at will. These routes can also be used as day outings visiting the bivouacs or refuges. They will be described starting with the most westerly.

Descent 1:
BIVOUAC GIRAUDO TO CERESOLE REALE

Grade: 3.

Time needed: 3¹/₄h for 1250m descent and 100m ascent to the
                    Colle Sia.

Comment: This is an attractive walk starting in the severe rock
                    scenery around the bivouac, traversing several alps
                    and then descending through forest to the valley.
                    Good views of the Levanna peaks on the Franco-
                    Italian frontier.

Route: From the bivouac, follow the route of section 2 as far as the
junction with the painted rock, where you go right and descend a
little into the level of the Alpi Breuillet. Cross the river and descend
gently among rocks then start to climb again going behind the
buildings of Alpi Loserai di Sotto and make a gentle climbing
traverse to the Colle Sia, an excellent viewpoint. A good path now
takes you down around the combe below to the Alpi Rana and soon
after you join the path of the Grand Traverse des Alps or GTA which
is waymarked with red and white flashes. This now descends
though the larch forest to Ceresole.

Note: If starting at Ceresole, the bivouac is referred to on signposts
as the Margherita rather than the Giraudo.

Historical note: *Ceresole Reale has a monument to a tragic event of the
Second World War which involved many British soldiers. They had
escaped from a prison camp at the capitulation of Italy and were supported
by the local partisans. It was decided that they, along with Italian partisans
and four Yugoslavian soldiers, should cross from Italy to Val d'Isère in
France to join the resistance there. The route chosen was up the Orco valley
and over the Col de la Galise. Unhappily, they were caught in a severe
blizzard which raged for six days and most perished near the Prariond
refuge in France. Alfred Southon, one of the two survivors, tells the story
in the book* Alpine Partisan. *Ceresole had a big remembrance event in
November 1995 on the 50th anniversary of the tragedy which was attended
by many notables, including a representative of the British Embassy.*

*There are other monuments to those who lost their lives, one on top of
the Col de la Galise and one one near the Prariond refuge.*

The Col de'la Galise was a regular smuggling route between the two wars this century. Salt went to Italy, and tobacco to France. This profitable trade also gave employment to customs officials and so was doubly beneficial!

Comment: Further east there are two paths marked on the maps which descend to Noasca, one from Alpi Gran Piano and one along the Vallone di Noasca.

Descent 2:
RIFUGIO PONTESE - VALLE DI PIANTONETTO - ROSONE

Grade: 3 initially, then simple track.

Time needed: 45m to the Telecchio dam then 1h 40m on road.

Comment: It is possible to drive to the Telecchio dam, despite there being no-road signs on the way. I was assured by the guardian that this was not forbidden. This gives easy access to this part of the national park.

Route: Follow a path from the refuge in a south-easterly direction over gently sloping ground then descend steeply in zigzags towards the head of the lake. This brings you to a track along the lakeside which goes to the dam, where the track climbs a little. This climb can be avoided by a path which cuts out the bends and leads directly to the top of the dam. The track down starts at this end of the dam.

Descent 3:
RIFUGIO POCCHIOLO MENEGHELLO TO
SAN GIACOMO AND ROSONE

Grade: 3

Time needed: 2h 40m. 4km of road to Rosone.

Comment: A steep and long descent in a valley which has, to an extent, been somewhat spoiled by the electricity works. Considering that the path leads to a refuge, it is not in a good state.

Route: Go to the south-eastern end of the dam, that is, the same side as the refuge, descend some steps and find a path which is waymarked and descends into the ravine below the dam. Cross a bridge and then a flat area before taking to the hillside and following the narrow path. This makes a steep descent through a band of cliffs using a series of grass ribs, and a gully, then descends more gently to the head of the Lago di Balme. This small lake is also artificial and completely blocks the valley. It is thus necessary to climb quite a way above the water to find a route through the cliffs. The path continues to descend quite steeply and you pass below the tree line. The path had suffered much wild boar damage when I passed this way and at times one had to cast around to find it. At about 1550m you come to a ruined hamlet called Lenzole and the path traverses right a little way through abandoned terraces. The path then plunges steeply through wooded gaps in the cliffs, so steeply that someone, long ago, has placed steps all the way down this section, a 300m staircase! It is still in quite good condition despite the ravages of the wild boar. You arrive in the hamlet of San Giacomo where you go left between the houses to reach the road. There is a signpost here indicating that this is the way to the refuge.

Botanical note: *In the latter part of the season it was usual to see clumps of* Dianthus pavonius *quite frequently along the way. This species is distinguished by having a deep pink flower with a buff reverse. It is normally short stemmed but in this region is a foot or more high, presumably to compete with the long grass in which it grows. Underfoot in the eastern part of the region there is a general cover of* Primula pedemontana, *though one would have to be early in the season to see it in flower. Finally, on the path up to the Rif. Pontese you may see growing in the cliffs above the path, the great white plumes of a saxifrage which I suspect is* Saxifraga cotyledon.

Some Shorter Walks

When making a detailed exploration of a region, as is needed to write such a guide as this, one is inevitably drawn to places which are not strictly on the long distance walks. Most of these turned out to be quite delightful detours and it would be wrong not to describe them. I shall give them centre by centre, starting at La Thuile and working east.

Glossary of equivalent names and spellings
Tête or Testa d'Arpy, d'Arpi, d'Arc
Lac d'Arpy or Arpi
Colle della Croce, de la Croix, de Becuit
Lago di Pietra Rossa, de la Pierre Rouge
Pointe Rousse, Punta Rossa
Tormotta, Tornotta
L. di Fond (o)
Col de Vaudet, Rocher Blanc, di Suessa
Alp Sey (i) vaz
Punta or Pointe or Col, Rossa or Rouge

SHORTER WALKS FROM LA THUILE
All the walks are on map IGC No.107 and the Bassa Serra walk is also shown in IGN TOP25 No.3531ET. See Map 13 (p110).

Walk A:
TÊTE D'ARPY, LAC D'ARPY, LAGO DI PIETRA ROSSA AND COL CROCE

Approach: From La Thuile take the road past the hamlets of Thovex and Buic and drive to the Colle San Carlo. Just past the top of the col there is parking and also the Hotel Genzianella which specialises in polenta dishes.
Comment: Four outings are possible from here and will be described in ascending order of difficulty.

TÊTE D'ARPY

Grade: 1.

Time needed: ¹/₂h there and back but allow plenty of time for the view.

Comment: As a walk this is trivial, but it takes you along a good track to a viewpoint which has one of the best of all views of the Mt Blanc range, with Courmayeur and Entrèves at the foot of the mountain. Definitely not to be missed on a good day.

Route: Go between the hotel and a ruined barracks and follow the track straight on, keeping right at a junction, to reach the edge of a cliff which forms the grand stand. The point is named Testa d'Arc on the IGC map.

LAC D'ARPY

Grade: 1.

Time needed: ³/₄h to get there, where you will tend to linger for a while.

Comment: A longer walk on a good track through larch woods whose colours in autumn defy belief. Rather more than 100m of climbing is involved but the slope is gentle and the way is liberally provided with wooden seats. The environs of the lake can best be described as the local "Tarn Hows". Good views of the Grandes Jorasses.

Route: A track goes off from the road across from the hotel and leads without incident to the main lake which appears suddenly as you surmount a little headland. The outlet of the lake makes a fine waterfall. It is possible to walk right round the lake as bridges have been provided over the streams at its foot and a little above its head. There are also some pretty satellite lakes near the head. Return the same way, or use the next route to make a round trip.

COL CROCE

Grade: 2 for the track up, 3 for the path down to Lac d'Arpy.

Time needed: 1h 45m to the col. A gently graded path.

Comment: A little more demanding but with excellent views of the Mt Blanc range and also of the mountains around the Col du Petit St Bernard. *Gentian brachyphilla* was in flower in October.

Route: Start as for Lac d'Arpy but go right when a junction is reached signposted to Col Croce. A good track ascends gently through many hairpin bends, gaining height gradually. Higher up there are a couple of places where stones have fallen on the track and narrowed it a little. Eventually the track narrows to a good path which traverses the hillside to bring you to the col, where there are extensive mining remains. The return can be made the same way, or there is a path which descends to La Thuile, though I have not done this. Better, perhaps, is to return via Lac d'Arpy. Go back a little along the path and turn sharp right below an abandoned building. There are evident waymarks. Follow the path down a little until an obvious path descends on the left. Take this down to the lake and return as for the previous walk.

LAGO DI PIETRA ROSSA

Grade: 4.

Approach: Walk up to Lac d'Arpy as already described.

Time needed: 1h 40m up from lake.

Comment: A much more serious undertaking than the other walks described. It takes you out of the beauty of the Lac d'Arpy into a much more severe mountain landscape which makes an almost shocking contrast.

Route: There is an obvious track which climbs into the combe ahead with the Torrent d'Arpy on its left. Either follow this or cross the torrent using the bridge above the head of the lake and follow a steep footpath on the other side of the torrent. If using the track, follow this to its end then cross scree to join the path. This climbs to a level spot then makes for the left-hand edge of the cliffs ahead where the rocks are more broken. You take a line more or less straight up over one or two awkward steps where there is some exposure, then up a broken groove onto a wide, gently sloping ledge. The rock wall ahead is broken on the right by a raked gully which is quite obvious and slopes up to the right. Cross the terrace to the foot of the rake, following easy ground with the help of cairns and yellow waymarks. Climb the rake on scree to a wide, flat terrace where you turn sharp left and follow a more or less horizontal path which climbs to the rocky bar retaining the lake, passing a red painted rock near the top. Return by the same route.

Walk B:
COLLE DI BASSA SERRA

The traverse of the Colle di Bassa Serra is part of the Via Alta 4 and is described in stage 6 of this walk, the approach being made via the Vallone del Breuil. The walk to the col makes a fine day's outing and can be made even more so if you return on the high ledge which runs parallel with the Vallone and behind the Pointe Rousse and the Tormotta.

Grade: 3 with bits of 4.

Approach: If walking from La Thuile follow the VA4 route to La Cretaz and the track and path to near Plan Veyle. If driving, follow the road to the Col du Petit St Bernard and park on the side road near Lago Verney. From here a track, rather cut up by cattle, takes you down to Le Balmette whence you climb to above Plan Veyle.

Time needed: 4h from Cretaz to col. $2^{1/}4$h from col to Lago Verney. $^{3/}4$h from lake to Cretaz.

Comment: The architecture of the Vallone del Breuil is a little unusual. It appears to be a short valley with high mountains to the north-east and high cliffs to the south west, the valley head being closed by these cliffs. Not visible is a high ledge which runs behind the cliffs and a great, shallow bowl which forms the true head of the valley. Once on this upper level you are within sight of the glaciers below the Franco-Italian frontier ridge and in much wilder country. The circuit makes a very worthwhile outing with some sections without path and a view of the omnipresent Mt Blanc from the col.

Route: From the track above Plan Veyle a path is signposted (number O10) climbing back to the right. A little way up this is a junction left which takes you along the right-hand side of the Vallone del Breuil. This leads steadily up to near the buildings of Entre Deux Eaux whence you climb quite quickly to a little reservoir, then start to traverse left to get above the apparent head of the valley. The cliffs across the valley form an impressive backdrop to this part of the walk, as do the several waterfalls. The path takes you over a little col and down onto the floor of the bowl which forms the real valley head. A good path climbs steadily almost straight ahead and takes you without difficulty to the Colle di Bassa Serra which is a level, roomy place.

Return: By the same path, or, better, using the shelf behind the Tormotta. Descend using the approach path. Below you on the right will be seen a tarn marked as 2525m on the map. Make for this, leaving the path at any convenient point, and arranging to make a smooth descent over easy ground. Pass the lake on its right and follow a shallow valley down to a flat alluvial area at about 2440m. It is essential not to follow the stream which goes over the cliffs into the lower part of the valley but to keep a low ridge between this and yourselves. On the other side of the alluvial area you will see a big moraine on the right and low grassy ridges straight ahead. Cross to the grass and climb directly at first but then tend right to reach moraine through which a cairned path takes you to the left. There is an attractive lake below the Tormotta and you keep above this and make for a rounded, grassy slope above. Once on this, a path suddenly appears and leads you on up a shallow valley, then crosses a couple of ridges, with a little scrambling, and finally takes you down, then up, to a col behind the Pointe Rousse at about 2600m. A good path descends the other side in zigzags and at the second big, left-hand bend a path will be seen traversing right across scree, making for a gap in low cliffs ahead. Cross to and pass through this, then follow ribs of mixed grass and rock down to a little tarn at 2280m. From there descend the slopes above Lago Verney to the lake.

The path from the col behind the Pointe Rousse is shown on the map as descending all the way to the lake. I have tried to follow this path and found that it just disappears in its upper part and that the lower part is very cut up by cattle, and is hence awkward.

Comment: *Lago Verney has a place in local French history. It used to be the custom that in times of great drought, the inhabitants of the village of Séez, at the foot of the Col du Petit St Bernard, on the Fench side, would make a pilgrimage to the lake, carrying a cross. This would be dipped in the lake, whereupon, one is told, the drought would immediately be broken. The new International Frontier set up on the creation of the state of Italy in 1860 impeded this custom, though it was not totally abandoned until after 1923.*

Walk C:
COL DA LA SEIGNE TO COLLE DI CHAVANNES

Comment:	This is in itself incomplete as a walk but is given as it provides a route connecting the Tour of Mt Blanc with the Via Alta, or another entry into the region from France. It is also an alternative approach to the Colle di Chavannes from the Vallon de la Lex Blanche, via the Col de la Seigne.
Approach:	It will be assumed that you are on the Col de la Seigne, having arrived from the Italian side, or from the French side via Les Chapieux.
Grade:	3.
Time needed:	1h.

Route: Looking towards the Colle di Chavannes it will be seen that there is a distinct shelf below the col which extends almost the whole way to the Col de la Seigne. Go right towards this ledge and follow paths just below it. Descend about 50m and eventually a path will be found which traverses horizontally, becoming more exposed as it proceeds, and takes you near to a gully and stream which runs down from the ledge. A narrow path ascends beside the gully in zigzags and takes you onto the ledge beside the stream. Cross this and then grass to the foot of scree, taking a diagonal line more or less directly towards the col. Make an ascending traverse left across the scree to a point below and to the right of the col. The path then becomes a little broken but leads to the col without any real difficulty.

SHORTER WALKS FROM VALGRISENCHE

The walks are best covered by the Italian 1:50,000 series of maps though much of the Tour of the Archeboc is on the IGN TOP25 3532ET.

Walk A:
PLANAVAL TO LAGO DI FONDO

Approach: The route starts at Planaval.

Comment: This is part of the crossing using the Colle di Planaval. It is an attractive walk in its own right. However early you start, there will always be fishermen there already.

Grade: 4.

Time needed: $3^{1/}4$h for 900m ascent. See Map 12 (p106).

Route: Follow the road through the hamlet of Planaval and continue in the direction of La Clusaz and Baulen, the latter being a good viewpoint. At La Clusaz there are two hairpin bends and a path goes off left just above the second bend. Note that there is limited parking near this point. The path makes a climbing traverse below cliffs with some quite airy sections, then climbs steeply through meadow until a level spot is reached near the river. You soon swing right to follow one branch of the river and climb into an upper valley where you pass the buildings of the Baracche di Fondo. Ahead the big gap of the Passo or Colle di Planaval is visible and a whole series of snowy summits of the Rutor group. A path junction with signpost appears

Mt Emilius from above Planaval

soon after and you take the right fork, a good path which climbs through rocky barriers to bring you quickly to the lake in its grand mountain setting. Picnicking and fishing seem to be the main occupations here, understandably so.

Return: by the same route.

Walk B:
THE TOUR OF THE ARCHEBOC OR ORMELUNE

This walk was, as far as I know, first proposed as a walk starting in and returning to France, though I see no reason why it should not be done from Italy! It takes two to three days and passes through a wide variety of scenery. The names provide a challenge. Two cols are crossed, the Col du Mont and the Col du Rocher Blanc, both names given from the French side of the ridge. The second col has also been named from the Italian side as the Col du Vaudet after the alp in Valgrisenche. In addition it has the name Colle di Suessaz which is apparently of Italian origin. The Archeboc itself also has a

143

confused nomenclature. To the Savoyards this is the name of the highest point with a subsidiary peak, the Ormelune to the south-east. The name of the whole group tends to be Ormelune, with variations, on the Italian maps but the term Archeboc also appears.

Approach: Drive or walk from Valgrisenche village to Surier at the head of Lago di Beauregard.

Comment: The tour can be done in either direction. It will be described in the anticlockwise direction.

Grade: Mostly 3 but the descent to the Rif. Bezzi should count as 4. See Map 17.

Section1. Surier to the Refuge de l'Archeboc

Time needed: 4h 40m. Ascent 850m and descent 607m.

Route: From Surier walk up the road and take the turning to Grande Alpage, then follow the track to Alpi Revera Basse. Pass the buildings and shortly after go left, down to the stream which is crossed by a bridge. Now make a climbing traverse on a good path to a ridge which is climbed in zigzags, then more steadily to the col where there may be some *névé*. An approach to the left seems best. The descent from the col is made on a good path which goes to the left of a ridge, then swings down in big zigzags to La Motte and the Refuge de l'Archeboc.

Section 2: Refuge de l'Archeboc to Le Monal

Time needed: 3¹/₄h. A gentle descent of 550m followed by a gentle ascent of 350m with much almost level ground.

Route: Below the refuge there are hayfields and across these, to the left as you descend from the Col du Mont, you can see a small pond on a little rise. Cross to this and find a path which crosses Les Savonnes and continues over moor, then through forest to join a track. The path is waymarked with red. Follow the track to a point at 1483m (or take paths which go a little higher) and then climb to the hamlet of Le Planay dessous and on to Le Planay dessus. Here,

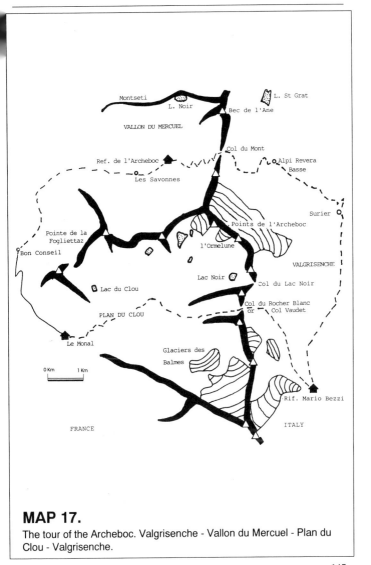

MAP 17.

The tour of the Archeboc. Valgrisenche - Vallon du Mercuel - Plan du Clou - Valgrisenche.

go through the centre of the village and follow a green track through fields to join a road just below a small chapel. Turn left and follow the road which leads to a ski piste. Follow this up a little, under a chair lift, and join another road on a bend and continue to the hamlet of Bon Conseil. Soon after the hamlet, the road becomes a track which is followed all the way to Le Monal. Parts of the track can be avoided on paths but avoid taking a left fork to Plan Bois.

Comment: Access by car to Le Monal is restricted and the hamlet is preserved much as it was in the pre car age. One of its buildings, on your right, has been converted into a refuge.

Section 3: Le Monal to Rifugio Bezzi and Surier

Time needed: 5h for 960m of ascent and 570m of descent as far as the Bezzi. Add another $1^1/_2$h for the descent to Surier.

Route: Continue through Le Monal, keeping right in the hamlet and climbing a little on a track. A path takes to the slope on the left and takes you up through woods to an open bowl below a track. Climb up right to this and follow it left over a sort of prow and then up to a rounded ridge overlooking the large plain called the Plan du Clou. Descend to and cross this, keeping the river on the left until you reach a bridge which is crossed and the track now takes you up to the chalets at Les Balmes. The path ahead goes to the Col du Lac Noir. A path is signposted right to the Col du Rocher Blanc. Take this, or go a little higher above the Balmes chalets before going right, a route which is perhaps a little less steep. Go round the end of the ridge into the valley leading to the col and follow a path which becomes a little vague but which covers easy enough ground. You aim for a small, V shaped valley below the col which has a path on its left and then start a steep pull up the final slopes below our multi-named col. The descent into the Grapillon valley on the other side is easy enough and takes you beside a shallow lake which may well be dried up, on faint paths. Here you meet a well marked path which descends from the Italian side of the Col du Lac Noir and follow this down, then across the stream. The path now makes a gently descending traverse almost due south over grassy slopes between bands of cliff. The spot is quite exposed and a couple of awkward glacier streams have to be crossed. You eventually arrive across the Dora Valgrisenche from the rifugio. A beam across another stream has to be negotiated and then a bridge across the main river. Go left to the rifugio. It is worth stopping to sample the food and the view of the valleyhead.

If continuing, pass the refuge and descend on a mostly good path, quite steeply, into the valley. Once past this section you are on track all the way to Surier.

SHORTER WALKS FROM PONT AND COL DEL NIVOLET

Pont is a busy centre in summer and there are several walks possible for anyone staying there. The environs of the Col del Nivolet are also busy, especially at weekends since the place is easily accessible by car from Turin and there is also a bus to the col on Sundays. As always, it is not too difficult to distance oneself from car borne crowds in the mountains. There are corners of great beauty and views of great majesty here for those who venture a little higher.

Walk A:
CIRCUIT OF PONT - GRAN COLLET -
CROIX D'AROLLEY - PONT

Grade: 3. A well positioned path on a steep hillside.

Time needed: Pont to col 3h, height gain 873m. Return to Pont 2h 20m. To Col del Nivolet also 2h 20m with 200m height gain. See Map 14 (p118).

Comment: This can be made either a round trip or used as an alternative route between Pont and the Col del Nivolet. It is a little-frequented route but has fine views of the glaciers and mountains around the Grand Paradis.

Ascent: From Pont, walk through the campsite on level ground and pick up a good path waymarked O2 which runs parallel with the river. Follow this until you are opposite a long, low building on the other side of the river. A path goes off right here, waymarked O2a,

147

and zigzags steeply up the hillside. This very cleverly works its way through bands of cliffs until you reach the level terrace of the Alp de Seyvaz where there is a memorial cross. The path makes a climbing traverse behind the chalet and then strikes more or less straight up in a direction which seems somewhat doubtful. The waymarks persist and the path is also well cairned. After one or two big steps the angle eases and the gap of the col ahead can be sensed. Cross a little hollow on scree on the right or on a path on the left and quickly arrive in a bowl whose far wall forms the last difficulty of the ascent. Climb fine scree to the lowest point which is to the right.

Descent: Follow scree down to a level area where the path is traced relatively lightly. Cross this until the angle steepens again and a good path takes you through rocks to the Alp du Gran Collet. If returning to Pont, go right and follow a wide highway of a path over level ground at first and then descend gently through rocks until you reach the Croix d'Arolley. Here one is suddenly confronted with a very steep descent, though a good path leads you down in zigzags back to Pont. If making for either of the refuges (Chivasso or Savoia), turn left and follow the valley bottom, climbing slowly to the road which is reached a little before the larger of the Lagi del Nivolet. The Savoia is on the right, near this lake, and the Chivasso is further on near the Col del Nivolet, and is visible from the road. For a view over the Lagi Agnel and Serru, walk a little further along the road to a belvedere. The waymarking in the valley is Δ4 and O3.

Walk B:
RIFUGIO VITTORIO EMANUELE AND THE CIRCUIT VIA RIFUGIO CHABOD

See Map 14 (p118).

To Rif. V. Emanuele:

Grade:	2. A much used path.
Time needed:	2h 45m from Pont to refuge.
Comment:	A wide path which takes you close to the snows around the Gran Paradiso itself. A pleasant outing.

Ascent: From the parking area at Pont cross the river and follow a level path south. A long, low building is passed and the path enters woods, crossing two new bridges. It then starts to climb in zigzags through the woods, then on open hillside to arrive at the large nissen-hut shaped refuge. It is possible to walk further to the edge of the glaciers.

Descent: By the same route or, with more difficulty, via Rif. Chabod - see below.

Continuation to Rif. Chabod (2750m):

Grade: 3.

Time needed: $2^{1}/_2$ to 3h. This is a balcony route but goes up and down with some awkward patches. The 5km distance is very misleading.

Route: Descend a little from the V. Emanuele to a signpost indicating the way to the Chabod. Follow the narrow path which continues to descend a little and takes a tortuous way through big rocks. Eventually this joins a second path which climbs from the Pont - V, Emanuele path and continues to traverse the hillside. Cross mixed terrain including a series of three moraine ridges. One comes close here to the Glacier of Lavaciau, though this appears to have retreated above the level marked on the maps. As a consequence, the path also seems to go higher than shown on the maps, particularly on the 1:50,000 version. The Torrente Costa Savolere is crossed by a bridge and one joins the way up to the Chabod near the last hairpin below the refuge.

Descent: Either by the route used for the ascent or directly to the valley by the path joined near the refuge. I have not used this path but it is broad and much frequented, even by families with young children, and can, I think, be recommended with confidence. You arrive in the valley below Alpage Pravieux where there is a big, much used car park and an enormous notice advertising Refuge Chabod. This of course is an alternative way up to the refuge which should take a little over 3 hours.

Walk C:
RIFUGIO CHABOD TO COLLE OVEST GRAN NEYRON

Grade: Initially 3, then 4 to col.

Time needed: 1h 40m to the col, though the going is rough in the higher part of the route and at times you will have to pick your way. See Map 8 (p78).

Comment: The crossing of this col is one of the harder parts of the Via Alta 4. The approach to and return from the col is a fine walk through some wild country and is within the reach of most experienced walkers.

Approach: It is assumed that you will start from and return to the Rif. Chabod.

Ascent: A path goes up behind the refuge, to the left, across open pastures and gaining only a little height at first. It takes you around some gullies and then climbs directly for the rock wall of the Punta Money. To avoid a collision it then turns sharp right and climbs in a traverse along the foot of this wall. A big combe appears into which you climb steeply and then traverse around on big blocks. The path is not always evident and the yellow waymarks are very helpful. The path continues along difficult ground with the ridge always on the left. A small bent tower on the ridge ahead marks the approximate position of the gap you are aiming for. Eventually you will see an arrow directing you upwards and which tells you to deviate from the apparent good track visible ahead. A short scramble leads you to the col and its breathtaking view down. Note that the 1:25,000 map shows the path as crossing the ridge too soon whereas the 1:50,000 map shows it as crossing a little further on than the col. There will however be no doubt as to when you are there since there is an obvious chain down the far side.

Descent: Necessarily by the same route.

Walk D:
LAGI DJOUAN AND LAGO NERO FROM EAUX ROUSSES

Grade: 3.

Time needed: 3h 20m for 1000m of ascent. See Map 7 (75).

Comment: This is a very pleasant and popular outing which follows part of stage 3 of the Via Alta 2, where the route is described in reverse. The path starts behind the hotel at Eaux Rousses.

FROM THE COL DEL NIVOLET

Several excursions are possible in the day from the Col del Nivolet, both short and long. To walk up to the Pian del Rosset from the Refuge Savoia is an excellent outing for the not too fit. It involves about 200m of ascent and takes you to an undulating plateau surrounded by mountains and dotted with azure lakes of all sizes. Lakes Rosset and Leità are the largest and with a little more effort you can visit the small lakes beside the path to Col Rosset or see the view of the Gran Paradiso beyond the Lagi di Trebecchi from the path to Col Leynir. Some longer outings follow:

Walk E:
COL ROSSET

Grade: 3.

Time needed: 2h to the col.

Route: Pass between lakes Rosset and Leità on a good path, then climb a steep slope in zigzags to arrive in a little valley below the Punta Rosset. The path climbs the steep wall below the col in many zigzags to reach the spacious summit.

Comment: This route is part of the VA4.

Walk F:
COL LEYNIR

Grade: 4.

Time needed: 2h 20m to the col.

Comment: This is given as an alternative for stage 2 of the VA4.

Route: Take a path which passes to the east of Lago Rosset and climbs steadily above it on a broad ridge. The path then zigzags up the open hillside ahead and traverses into a wild valley where the going is relatively level. You come to a minor col and descend a little into the Vallone Leynir. The path now climbs a steep slope in a series of zigzags, crossing sections of steep *névé* as it does (ski pole almost essential) to arrive on the col directly above the glacier of Vaudalettaz.

Return: By the same route.

Walk G:
COLLE DEL NIVOLETTA

Grade: 4.

Time needed: 2h 20m to the col.

Comment: an alternative crossing on stage 2 of the VA4 and also the recommended route for the early part of the GTGP. Technically much more difficult than the last walk.

Route: Pass to the west of Lago Leità, avoiding a path which goes left and continuing to the end of the ridge above, which is climbed, either by a small gully on the right, or over the shoulder on the left. This brings you onto a broad ledge which is followed until the path climbs *névé* to the Colle Basei. The Colle del Nivoletta is along the broad ridge on your right, though it is not necessary to go all the way to enjoy the magnificent views. Again, a ski pole is useful on this route.

Return: by the same route.

Walk H:
COL DE LA TERRA

Grade: 3.

Time needed: 2h to the col.

Comment: Part of the GTGP, a pleasant walk.

Route: Start at the lake marked as 2461m altitude on the south side of the Col del Nivolet, where there is an obtrusive power line. The path goes south of the lake and traverses slopes above the upper Orco valley. Eventually, you start to make a climbing traverse of scree and cross a gully below the col, making for the slopes of the Punta Rocchetta where you swing sharp left and quickly gain the col. To see Lago Lillet, it is necessary to descend a little on the far side of the col.

Return: by the same route.

SHORT WALKS FROM VALNONTEY

This is a much frequented place since there is plenty of accommodation and some magnificent scenery. Most of the walks are sections of the Via Alta but there is one in addition:

Walk A:
COL DE LA ROUSSE

Comment:	This walk takes you to Rif. V. Sella and on to a remote col. You are very likely to see ibex.
Grade:	2 to refuge, 4 to col.
Time needed:	3h for 889m height gain to the refuge. To the col a further 2h for 611m climbing. See Map 8 (78).

Ascent: Cross the bridge in Valnontey and follow the road left to a parking area whence a path goes off on the left, passes the alpine garden, and makes for the slope behind, which looks impregnable but in fact conceals an almost "jeepable" track. This climbs in comfortable zigzags and gives good views of the Torrente Gran Lauson. A bridge near the top of this steep section leads to alpine pastures and chalets but you keep the river on your left and continue up the wall of the V shaped valley. A quick climb at the end of this brings you to a level area with the refuge set back, towards the river. There is a bar/restaurant here also and much tourism. Waymarks Δ2 or O18 on to Col de la Rousse.

Comment: The next section is a steep path to a col overlooked by the spires of the Punta Rossa. A series of paths on the other side is said to lead down without difficulty to the valley of Cogne via either Vallone del Pousset or Vallone di Vermianaz. In late July 1994 the path above the waterslide was lined by tufts of the gentian blue "forget-me-not" known as the King of the Alps (*Eritrichium nanum*), growing atypically in turf. A few plants also grow on the approach to Col Lauson but on the rock.

Ascent: Follow the path to the Col Lauson until an obvious path is reached which leads off back to the right. A rock carries the legend 'Col de la Rousse' and 'Col Nero' and avoids all doubt. The path climbs a steep grass slope in zigzags making for a rather doubtful looking gap in the cliffs above. This turns out not to be as difficult as it looks and is passed by walking through a waterslide over screes. Anyone wearing trainers may well get wet feet! After a stiff climb the path meanders among the flowers but then makes steeply for the col. Waymarks O26b infrequent.

Return: by the same route.

Walk B:
COL LAUSON

Grade:	4. The top is both slippery and exposed.
Time needed:	2¹/₂h from Rif. V. Sella with almost 700m of ascent. This is the highest walker's col in the region.
Comment:	This is part of both VA2 and VA4.

Route: Climb to the Rif. V. Sella as described for walk A. Follow up to the rock where a path to the right is signposted to Col de la Rousse but continue left on a path which climbs into a bowl, then traverses scree to the right of the valley ahead. Towards the top the path steepens and brings you to a false top, where a chain is installed. This is followed around the top of a gully to the real top which is only a little higher.

Return: by the same route.

Walk C:
THE HERBETET CHALETS

Grade: 2.

Time needed: 3h from Valnontey to the chalets.

Comment: Part of stage 2 of the VA4.

Route: Follow the track up Valnontey, past the hamlet of Valmianaz to the Pont d'Erfaulet. Cross this and follow a path through woods, then zigzag up open hillside to reach the chalets where there is a water supply. Picnic here, or go a little further on to the right to the Pian di Ressello, though parts of this path are exposed. The path becomes progressively more difficult beyond the Pian di Ressello.

Return: by the same route.

CICERONE GUIDE BOOKS
LONG DISTANCE WALKS

There are many Cicerone guides to long distance walks in Britain or abroad, which make a memorable holiday or shorter break.

GENERAL TREKKING

THE TREKKER'S HANDBOOK *Thomas R. Gilchrist* Everything a trekker needs to know, from gear to health. *ISBN 1 85284 205 9 A5 size £10.99*

FAR HORIZONS Adventure Travel for All! *Walt Unsworth* From European trails to Himalayan treks; from deserts of Central Asia to jungles of Borneo; from wildwater rafting to gorges of the Yangtse. Based on the author's wide experience of this growing form of holiday travel. *ISBN 1 85284 228 8 160pp A5 size £8.99*

LAKE DISTRICT & NORTHERN ENGLAND

THE CUMBRIA WAY AND ALLERDALE RAMBLE *Jim Watson.* A guide to two popular Lake District long distance walks. *ISBN 1 85284 242 3 £6.99*

THE EDEN WAY *Charlie Emett* Through a romantic part of Cumbria. Breaks into sections by using the popular Settle-Carlisle railway. *ISBN 1 85284 040 4 192pp £5.99*

IN SEARCH OF WESTMORLAND *Charlie Emett* A walk around the old county. Full of rich anecdotes and history. *ISBN 0 902363 66 2 200pp £5.50*

WALKING ROUND THE LAKES *John & Anne Nuttall* The ideal walk encompassing all the major summits, yet with high and low level alternatives. *ISBN 1 85284 099 4 240pp £6.99*

WESTMORLAND HERITAGE WALK *Chris Wright and Mark Richards* A circular walk around the old county. *ISBN 0 902363 94 8 256pp PVC cover £7.99*

THE DALES WAY *Terry Marsh* A practical handbook to a very popular walk. With Accommodation Guide. *ISBN 1 85284 102 8 136pp £5.99*

THE DOUGLAS VALLEY WAY *Gladys Sellers* Through the heart of Lancashire. *ISBN 1 85284 073 0 72pp £4.99*

HADRIAN'S WALL Vol 1: The Wall Walk *Mark Richards* Mark conducts you along the wall, accompanied by his skilful maps and sketches. *ISBN 1 85284 128 1 224pp £7.99*

THE ISLE OF MAN COASTAL PATH *Aileen Evans* The Raad ny Foillan path encircles the island; the Herring Way and the Millennium Way are also described. *ISBN 0 902363 95 6 144pp £5.99*

LAUGHS ALONG THE PENNINE WAY *Pete Bogg* Anyone who has struggled through the bogs of the Pennine Way will identify with the humour of this cartoon book. An ideal gift. *ISBN 0 902363 97 2 104pp £2.99*

A NORTHERN COAST TO COAST WALK *Terry Marsh* The most popular LD walk in Britain. Includes accommodation guide. *ISBN 1 85284 126 5 280pp £7.99*

THE RIBBLE WAY *Gladys Sellers* From sea to source close to a junction with the Pennine Way. *ISBN 1 85284 107 9 112pp £5.99*

THE REIVER'S WAY *James Roberts* 150 miles around Northumberland. *ISBN 1 85284 130 3 112pp £5.99*

THE TEESDALE WAY *Martin Collins* A new walk which follows the Tees from its source to the sea. 100 miles, 8 stages. *ISBN 1 85284 198 2 112pp £7.99*

WALKING THE CLEVELAND WAY & THE MISSING LINK *Malcolm Boyes* Circular tour of the North York Moors, including some of our finest coastline. *ISBN 1 85284 014 5 144pp £5.99*

WHITE PEAK WAY *Robert Haslam* An 80-mile walk through the Derbyshire Dales with full details of youth hostels, pubs etc. *ISBN 1 85284 056 0 96pp £4.99*

WEEKEND WALKS IN THE PEAK DISTRICT *John & Anne Nuttall* Magnificent weekend outings illustrated with John's fine drawings. *ISBN 1 85284 137 0 296pp £9.99*

THE VIKING WAY *John Stead* From Barton-upon-Humber to Rutland Water: *ISBN 1 85284 057 9 172pp £5.99*

WALES & THE WELSH BORDER

THE LLEYN PENINSULA COASTAL PATH *John Cantrell.* Starting at Caernarfon the coastal path goes round the peninsula to Porthmadog following the old Bardsey Pilgrims' route. Described for walkers and cyclists, with additional day walks. *ISBN 1 85284 252 0*

WALKING OFFA'S DYKE PATH *David Hunter* Along the Welsh Marches, 170 miles from Chepstow to Prestatyn. *ISBN 1 85284 160 5 224pp £8.99*

THE PEMBROKESHIRE COASTAL PATH *Dennis R. Kelsall* One of Britain's most beautiful paths. includes accommodation guide. *ISBN 1 85284 186 9 200pp £9.99*

SARN HELEN *Arthur Rylance & John Cantrell* The length of Wales in the footsteps of the Roman legions. *ISBN 1 85284 101 X 248pp £8.99*

WALKING DOWN THE WYE *David Hunter* 112 mile walk from Rhayader to Chepstow. *ISBN 1 85284 105 2 192pp £6.99*

A WELSH COAST TO COAST WALK- Snowdonia to Gower *John Gillham* An ideal route for backpackers, away from waymarked trails. *ISBN 1 85284 218 0 152pp £7.99*

SOUTHERN ENGLAND

THE COTSWOLD WAY *Kev Reynolds* A guide to this popular walk. *ISBN 1 85284 049 8 168pp £6.99*

THE GRAND UNION CANAL WALK *Clive Holmes* Along the canal which links the Black Country to London, through rural England *ISBN 1 85284 206 7 128pp £5.99*

THE KENNET & AVON WALK *Ray Quinlan* 90 miles along riverside and canal, from Westminster to Avonmouth, full of history, wildlife, delectable villages and pubs. *ISBN 1 85284 090 0 200pp £6.99*

AN OXBRIDGE WALK *J.A.Lyons* Over 100 miles linking the university cities of Oxford and Cambridge. *ISBN 1 85284 166 4 168pp £7.99*

THE SOUTHERN COAST-TO-COAST WALK *Ray Quinlan* The equivalent of the popular northern walk. 283 miles from Weston-super-Mare to Dover. *ISBN 1 85284 117 6 200pp £6.99*

THE SOUTH DOWNS WAY & THE DOWNS LINK *Kev Reynolds* A guide to these popular walks. *ISBN 1 85284 023 4 136pp £5.99*

SOUTH WEST WAY - A Walker's Guide to the Coast Path Vol.1 Minehead to Penzance *Martin Collins*
ISBN 1 85284 025 0 184pp PVC cover £8.99

Vol.2 Penzance to Poole *Martin Collins*
ISBN 1 85284 026 9 198pp PVC cover £8.99
Two volumes which cover the spectacular coastal path around Britain's south-west peninsula.

THE TWO MOORS WAY *James Roberts* 100 miles crossing Dartmoor, the villages of central Devon and Exmoor to the coast at Lynmouth. *ISBN 1 85284 159 1 100pp £5.99*

THE WEALDWAY & THE VANGUARD WAY *Kev Reynolds* Two LD walks in Kent, from the outskirts of London to the coast. *ISBN 0 902363 85 9 160pp £4.99*

SCOTLAND

THE WEST HIGHLAND WAY *Terry Marsh* A practical guide to this very popular walk. *ISBN 1 85284 235 0 £6.99*

IRELAND

THE IRISH COAST TO COAST WALK *Paddy Dillon* From Dublin and the Wicklows to Valencia Island on the Kerry coast, linking various trails. *ISBN 1 85284 211 3 £7.99*

FRANCE

THE BRITTANY COASTAL PATH *Alan Castle* The GR34, 360 miles takes a month to walk. Easy access from UK means it can be split into several holidays. *ISBN 1 85284 185 0 296pp £10.99*

THE CORSICAN HIGH LEVEL ROUTE - Walking the GR20 *Alan Castle* The most challenging of the French LD paths - across the rocky spine of Corsica. *ISBN 1 85284 100 1 104pp £5.99*

THE PYRENEAN TRAIL: GR10 *Alan Castle* From the Atlantic to the Mediterranean at a lower level than the Pyrenean High Route. 50 days but splits into holiday sections. *ISBN 1 85284 245 8 176pp £8.99*

THE ROBERT LOUIS STEVENSON TRAIL *Alan Castle* 140 mile trail in the footsteps of Stevenson's "Travels with a Donkey" through the Cevennes. *ISBN 1 85284 060 9 160pp £7.99*

TOUR OF MONT BLANC *Andrew Harper* One of the world's best walks - the circumnavigation of the Mont Blanc massif. *ISBN 1 85284 240 7 168pp PVC cover*

TOUR OF THE OISANS: GR54 *Andrew Harper* Around the massif, similar in quality to the Tour of Mont Blanc. *ISBN 1 85284 157 5 120pp PVC cover £9.99*

THE TOUR OF THE QUEYRAS *Alan Castle* 13 days across the mountains of the French Alps. Suitable for a first Alpine visit. *ISBN 1 85284 048 X 160pp £6.99*

TOUR OF THE VANOISE *Kev Reynolds* A circuit of one of the finest mountain areas of France. The second most popular mountain tour after the Tour of Mont Blanc. *ISBN*

WALKING THE FRENCH ALPS: GR5 *Martin Collins* The popular From Lake Geneva to Nice. Split into stages, each of which could form the basis of a good holiday. *ISBN 1 85284 051 X 160pp £8.99*

WALKING THE FRENCH GORGES *Alan Castle* 320 miles through Provence and Ardèche, includes the famous Verdon. *ISBN 1 85284 114 1 224pp £7.99*

WALKING IN THE TARENTAISE & BEAUFORTAIN ALPS *J.W. Akitt* Delectable mountains south of Mont Blanc includes the Vanoise National Park. 53 day walks, 5 tours between 2 and 8 days duration, plus 40 short outings. *ISBN 1 85284 181 8 216pp £9.99*

WALKS IN VOLCANO COUNTRY *Alan Castle* Two LD walks in Central France- the High Auvergne and Tour of the Velay - in a unique landscape of extinct volcanoes. *ISBN 1 85284 092 7 208pp £8.50*

THE WAY OF ST JAMES: GR65 *H.Bishop* French section of the pilgrim's route, across Massif Central from Le Puy to the Pyrenees. *ISBN 1 85284 029 3 96pp £5.50*

FRANCE/SPAIN

WALKS & CLIMBS IN THE PYRENEES *Kev Reynolds* Includes the Pyrenean High Level Route.. (3rd Edition) *ISBN 1 85284 133 8 328pp PVC cover £14.99*

SPAIN

WALKING IN MALLORCA *June Parker*. The 3rd edition takes account of rapidly changing conditions. Includes the classic multi-day walk through the backbone of the mountains. One of the great walking guides. *ISBN 1 85284 250 4*

THE MOUNTAINS OF CENTRAL SPAIN *Jacqueline Oglesby* Walks and scrambles in the Sierras de Gredos and Guadarrama which rise to 2600m and are snow capped for five months of the year. *ISBN 1 85284 203 2 312p £14.99*

THROUGH THE SPANISH PYRENEES: GR11 *Paul Lucia* A new long distance trail which mirrors the French GR10 but traverses much lonelier, wilder country *ISBN 1 85284 222 9 216pp £10.99*

WALKING IN THE SIERRA NEVADA *Andy Walmsley* Spain's highest mountain range, a wonderland for traveller and wilderness backpacker. Mountain bike routes are indicated. *ISBN 1 85284 194 X 160pp £8.99*

THE WAY OF ST JAMES: SPAIN *Alison Raju* The popular Pilgrim Road from the Pyrenees to Santiago de Compostela. *ISBN 1 85284 142 7 152pp £7.99*

SWITZERLAND including adjacent parts of France and Italy

ALPINE PASS ROUTE, SWITZERLAND *Kev Reynolds* Over 15 passes along the northern edge of the Alps, past the Eiger, Jungfrau and many other renowned peaks. *ISBN 1 85284 069 2 176pp £6.99*

CHAMONIX to ZERMATT The Walker's Haute Route *Kev Reynolds* In the shadow of great peaks from Mont Blanc to the Matterhorn. *ISBN 1 85284 215 6 176pp £7.99*

THE JURA: WALKING THE HIGH ROUTE *Kev Reynolds* **WINTER SKI TRAVERSES** *R.Brian Evans* The High

Route is a LD path along the highest crest of the Swiss Jura. In winter the area is a paradise for cross-country skiers. *ISBN 1 85284 010 2 192pp £6.99*

THE GRAND TOUR OF MONTE ROSA *C.J.Wright*
Vol 1 - Martigny to Valle della Sesia (via the Italian valleys) *ISBN 1 85284 177 X 216pp £14.99*
Vol 2 - Valle della Sesia to Martigny (via the Swiss valleys) *ISBN 1 85284 178 8 182pp £14.99* The ultimate alpine LD walk which encircles most of the Pennine Alps.

GERMANY, AUSTRIA & EASTERN EUROPE

GERMANY'S ROMANTIC ROAD A guide for walkers and cyclists *Gordon McLachlan* 423km past historic walled towns and castles of southern Germany . *ISBN 1 85284 233 4 208pp £9.99 (May)*

HUT TO HUT IN THE STUBAI ALPS *Allan Hartley* Two classic tours: The Stubai Rucksack Route and The Stubai Glacier Tour, each taking around 10 days. Easy peaks and good huts make it a good area for a first Alpine season. *ISBN 1 85284 123 0 128pp Card cover £6.99*

KING LUDWIG WAY *Fleur and Colin Speakman* Travels the Bavarian countryside from Munich to Füssen. King Ludwig was responsible for the fabulous castle of Neuschwanstein . *ISBN 0 902363 90 5 80pp £3.99*

MOUNTAIN WALKING IN AUSTRIA *Cecil Davies* Describes walks in 17 mountain groups, from single day to multi-day hut to hut excursions. *ISBN 1 85284 239 3 200pp*

WALKING IN THE BLACK FOREST *Fleur & Colin Speakman* Above the Rhine valley, the Westweg was Europe's first waymarked trail in 1900. *ISBN 1 85284 050 1 120pp £5.99*

SCANDINAVIA

WALKING IN NORWAY *Connie Roos* 20 walking routes in the main mountain areas from the far south to the sub arctic regions, all accessible by public transport. *ISBN 1 85284 230 X 200pp £10.99*

ITALY & SLOVENIA

ALTA VIA - HIGH LEVEL WALKS IN THE DOLO-MITES *Martin Collins* A guide to some of the most popular mountain paths in Europe - Alta Via 1 and 2. *ISBN 0 902363 75 1 160pp PVC cover £8.99*

THE GRAND TOUR OF MONTE ROSA *C.J.Wright* See entry under Switzerland

LONG DISTANCE WALKS IN THE GRAN PARADISO *J.W. Akitt.* Describes Alta Via 2 and the Grand Traverse of Gran Paradiso.. *ISBN 1 85284 247 4*

MEDITERRANEAN COUNTRIES

THE ATLAS MOUNTAINS *Karl Smith* Trekking in the mountains of north Africa. Practical and comprehensive. *ISBN 1 85284 032 3 136pp PVC cover £9.99*

CRETE OFF THE BEATEN TRACK *Bruce and Naomi Caughey* Short walks, mountain hikes, gorges, coves and beaches. Ruins of ancient civilizations abound. *ISBN 1 85284 019 6 152pp £7.99*

THE MOUNTAINS OF GREECE. A Walker's Guide *Tim Salmon* Hikes of all grades from a month-long traverse of

the Pindos to day hikes on the outskirts of Athens. *ISBN 1 85284 108 7 PVC cover £9.99*

THE MOUNTAINS OF TURKEY *Karl Smith* Over 100 treks and scrambles with detailed descriptions of the popular peaks. Includes Ararat. *ISBN 1 85284 161 3 184pp PVC cover £14.99*

TREKS AND CLIMBS in WADI RUM, JORDAN *Tony Howard.* The world's foremost desert climbing and trekking area.*ISBN 1 85284 135 4 252pp A5 Card cover £12.99*

THE ALA DAG, Climbs and Treks in Turkey's Crimson Mountains *O.B.Tüzel* The best mountaineering area in Turkey. *ISBN 1 85284 112 5 296pp PVC cover £14.99*

HIMALAYA

ANNAPURNA - A Trekker's Guide *Kev Reynolds* Includes Annapurna Circuit, Annapurna Sanctuary and Pilgrim's Trail, with lots of good advice. *ISBN 1 85284 132 X 184pp £8.99*

EVEREST - A Trekker's Guide *Kev Reynolds* The most popular trekking region in the Himalaya. Lodges, teahouse, permits, health - all are dealt with in this indispensible guide. *ISBN 1 85284 187 7 £8.99*

LANGTANG, GOSAINKUND & HELAMBU - A Trekker's Guide *Kev Reynolds* Popular area, easily accessible from Kathmandu. *ISBN 1 85284 207 5 £8.99*

ADVENTURE TREKS IN NEPAL *Bill O'Connor* *ISBN 1 85223 306 0 160pp large format £9.99*

OTHER COUNTRIES

MOUNTAIN WALKING IN AFRICA 1: KENYA *David Else* Detailed route descriptions and practical information. *ISBN 1 85365 205 9 A5 size £9.99*

TREKKING IN THE CAUCAUSUS *Yuri Kolomiets & Aleksey Solovyev* Hidden until recently behind the Iron Curtain. Included are the highest tops in Europe, the summits of Mt Elbrus. *ISBN 1 85284 129 X 224pp PVC cover £14.99*

ADVENTURE TREKS WESTERN NORTH AMERICA *Chris Townsend* *ISBN 1 85223 317 6 160pp large format £9.99*

CLASSIC TRAMPS IN NEW ZEALAND *Constance Roos* The 14 best long distance walks in both South and North Islands. *ISBN 1 85284 118 4 208pp PVC cover £14.99*

Printed by Carnmor Print & Design, London Road, Preston, Lancs. England